FOLLOWING GOD
CHRISTIAN LIVING
STUDY SERIES

An informative **6 WEEK BIBLE STUDY**
of life principles for today, to guide the church
and the Christian's walk.

Loving One Another

THE COMMUNITY GOD
WANTS US TO BE

AMG
PUBLISHERS

EDDIE RASNAKE

Following God

LOVING ONE ANOTHER: THE COMMUNITY GOD WANTS US TO BE

ISBN 13: 978-1-61715-531-4

Unless otherwise noted,
Scripture is taken from the *New American Standard Bible*®. Copyright © 1960, 1962, 1963,
1968, 1971, 1972, 1973, 1975, 1977, 1995, by The Lockman Foundation. Used by permission.
(www.Lockman.org)

Portions appear from *The Complete Word Study Old Testament*
Copyright © 1994 by AMG Publishers.
Used by permission.

Manuscript editing, text design, and layout by Rick Steele Editorial Services
http://steeleeditorialservices.myportfolio.com

Cover illustration by Daryle Beam/Bright Boy Design

Printed in the United States of America
2020 First Edition

I dedicate this book to my friends in the

"Crowded Table" fellowship—

a special group the Lord has raised up to love
those on the fringes who have been marginalized
in our world. We want the house of God to be
"a house with a crowded table, and a place by the
fire for everyone...everyone's a little broken, and
everyone belongs."

ACKNOWLEDGMENTS

Writing is always a synergistic activity for me. I am inspired by my home church—Woodland Park Baptist—who seek to honor the Lord, His Word, and His people. They were the guinea pigs for developing these ideas, and I am thankful for their heart for true community. Special thanks to Steve Turner and Amanda Jenkins at AMG Publishers for believing in this project and nurturing it along. As always, I am grateful for the skillful editing of Rick Steele in polishing the prose and catching my misteaks (oops)! A special thanks to my old friend and fellow author, Rick Shepherd, for his kind words and endorsement. Thanks to my wife whose love and patience keep me looking forward to coming home each day.

THE AUTHOR

Eddie Rasnake

EDDIE RASNAKE graduated with honors from East Tennessee State University. He and his wife, Michele, served seven years with Cru (formerly Campus Crusade for Christ) at the University of Virginia, James Madison University, and the University of Tennessee (as campus director). Eddie left Cru to join Wayne Barber at Woodland Park Baptist Church, where he still serves as Senior Associate Pastor. He has authored dozens of books and Bible studies and has published materials in Afrikaans, Albanian, German, Greek, Italian, Romanian, Russian, and Telugu. Eddie and his wife Michele live in Chattanooga, Tennessee.

PREFACE

The disciples ask Jesus about the signs of His coming and of the end of the age, and many of us are familiar with the signs He references in this conversation. He mentions wars and rumors of wars, famines, earthquakes, tribulation, and false prophets. Tucked in among these cataclysmic events is a sign that is often overlooked. He says in Matthew 24:12 that "most people's love will grow cold." In his last epistle before he was martyred, the apostle Paul warns that in the last days people will be "unloving" and "lovers of self" (2 Timothy 3:2–3). These end times signs seem to be all around us. Urbanization has left many people crowded with strangers yet feeling alone. A global economy and transient employment has moved many far away from the safety net of family and lifelong friends. Technology has distracted us and disconnected us from many of the real, face-to-face connections that used to make up our days. Social media has become a pseudo substitute for real friendships. While it can be easy to be pessimistic in the light of such seismic cultural shift, all is not hopeless. Against this dark backdrop, I believe the Lord has positioned His church to shine more brightly than ever. Because the love of God is within us, and the Spirit bonds us together, I believe that these last days may be the church's finest hour.

This book was born out of the oft repeated refrains of the New Testament we call the "One Another" commands—our Divine mandate to love deeply and to practice radically ordinary hospitality in a world that has forgotten the God who so loves them He gave His only begotten Son. Over the course of this Bible study, we will examine the entire list of "One Anothers" and seek to Apply them to our lives. I believe that living out biblical community is going to make the church more irresistible than ever as people who are love-starved come in contact with the love of God poured out through His people. *"By this everyone will know that you are my disciples, if you love one another"* (John 13:35).

Following HIm,

Eddie Rasnake

CONTENTS

LESSON 1

COMMUNITY MATTERS

The "Lone Ranger" is a fictional character who first appeared as an American radio program in the 1930's. The show proved to be a hit, and its success spawned a series of books, a long-running television show, and several movie adaptations. The basic plot involves a Texas Ranger who purportedly is the sole survivor of a group of six Rangers who were ambushed while in pursuit of a band of outlaws. A Native American named Tonto enters the story and finds this one Ranger barely alive. He cares for The Lone Ranger until his health is restored and then assists him in his quest for justice in the North American old west. The masked character is an endearing and enduring American icon, along with his sidekick, Tonto, and trusty horse, "Silver."

While the idea of a "Lone Ranger" has a romantic appeal, he is not a good model for how believers should approach living out their faith. Far too many Christians try to "go it alone." They may attend church services and worship in the larger gathering of believers— or they may simply avail themselves of technological ways to experience services. Maybe they listen on the radio or watch live-streaming gatherings via the internet. They see the importance of the content of evangelical worship without grasping the community side of Christianity. These "Lone Ranger" Christians live out the bulk of their faith as if it were a solo sport. The irony is that even the original Lone Ranger wasn't alone. He always had his friend Tonto with him.

> *"Lone Ranger" Christians live out the bulk of their faith as if it were a solo sport.*

A great many churches are evaluating themselves these days, trying to figure out why their attendance is shrinking. They may have great programs and lots of activity, but the common concern being voiced quite often is that what's missing is community. This shouldn't be surprising. Real, authentic community is going missing in our culture as a whole. While fifty years ago it was common to build close-knit relationships with our neighbors, in many areas people live in proximity and don't even know each other's names, let alone what is going on in each other's lives. Family units are fractured by rela- tional dysfunctions and job relocation logistics in a highly mobile and transient society.

Many people today feel isolated and alone. I believe this presents a great opportunity for reaching people for churches that do well at community, but it isn't happening as broadly as it should. Even in churches with great opportunities for community, not everyone is taking advantage and plugging in. Some believers just don't see the need.

In this first lesson, I want to tackle the problem of Lone Ranger Christians by looking at some very wise words. King Solomon of the Old Testament is history's wealthiest and wisest king. Because of his great intelligence, he could've thought he didn't need anyone else. Certainly, he was capable of making every decision by himself. With his tremendous wealth, he had the potential to depend on his own resources. If anyone could get away with flying solo, it was Solomon. Instead, he built a team of advisors around himself. He was wise enough to know that he didn't know it all and couldn't do it all. Listen to what he wrote near the end of his life in Ecclesiastes 4:9–12...

> *"Two are better than one because they have a good return for their labor. For if either of them falls, the one will lift up his companion. But woe to the one who falls when there is not another to lift him up. Furthermore, if two lie down together they keep warm, but how can one be warm alone? And if one can overpower him who is alone, two can resist him. A cord of three strands is not quickly torn apart."*

In these few short verses we find some pretty wise advice on why community matters —why we need to do life together as believers. In these verses, Solomon offers four illustrations from everyday life on why we shouldn't be "Lone Ranger" Christians and should instead learn to live in community with each other.

DAY ONE

IN COMMUNITY WE HAVE A GREATER SPIRITUAL IMPACT

Floyd H. Allport is regarded by most as the founder of social psychology as a scientific discipline, and rightly so. His 1924 book, *Social Psychology*, was the first of its kind, offering not just theories, but a systematically-built case for his ideas through experimentation and studying interpersonal human relationships. Some of the concepts had been around for a while as theories, but it was Allport's methodology that set him apart. From his early days at Harvard as a graduate student and later as a professor, to chairing the newly formed school for the social sciences at Syracuse University, to directing the first doctoral program for social psychology in the United States, he continued to shape this important academic field until his retirement in 1956. His ongoing contributions to both theory and research "marked the major avenues along which social psychology was to travel through its youth and early maturity. His pioneer efforts in methodology were so deep and broad that most of the methods in use today are refinements of his early work in group experimentation, field studies, attitude measurement, and behavioral observation"

("Allport, Floyd H." "International Encyclopedia of the Social Sciences." Encyclopedia. com. 7 Jan. 2019 <https://www.encyclopedia.com>).

> *"Two are better than one because they have a good return for their labor."* (Ecclesiastes 4:9)

One of Allport's groundbreaking studies, as he was working on his dissertation at Harvard, was on a comparison of the performance of individuals acting alone to that of acting in groups. Through his research in 1920 on the influence of the group upon association and thought, published in the *Journal of Experimental Psychology* (3:159-182), he showed empirically that a group of people working individually at the same table performed better on a whole range of tasks even though they weren't cooperating or competing. Just by being around other people, they accomplished more. While common sense suggests such a conclusion, Allport was able to validate through a scientific process, what Solomon states in Ecclesiastes 4:9 that *"Two are better than one because they have a good return for their labor."* In this first illustration, Solomon makes the point that your spiritual life and my spiritual life need the help, the encouragement, the support, the strength, and the example of others. We need Christian community because in community we have a greater spiritual impact.

📖 Read Mark 6:7 and Luke 10:1 in their context and reflect on what you see there.

_____

_____

_____

_____

_____

_____

_____

_____

Have you ever wondered why Jesus sent the disciples out by twos? Let me assure you, it wasn't a random thing. It's a simple principle really, and yet incredibly profound. Christianity is not a solo sport. Lest we are tempted to think that this principle was only for the twelve disciples, Luke 10 makes it clear that this practice was the norm for the broader group of followers as well. By sending the disciples out in this manner, Jesus provided them with both encouragement and accountability in their ministry tasks. It is easier to be brave with someone else than by ourselves. Together we can do what we might not do alone.

Examine Acts 13:1-5. Who made up the team of workers on the first missionary journey, and what does this passage add to our understanding of Jesus' principle?

DID YOU KNOW?
Return

The Hebrew word *sakar*, translated "return" in Ecclesiastes 4:9, has the idea of wages. It reminds us that as believers, we will be rewarded in heaven for our service on earth.

It is clear from this passage that world missions began as team sport. While we tend to associate the apostle Paul as a missionary, by the Holy Spirit's initiative he clearly had partners in his labors. This principle would remain his practice for the rest of his life. We see this evidenced in the fact that each of his epistles are identified as coming from Paul and others such as Silas or Sothsenes or such.

Some tasks require a partner (see-saw, tango, tennis)—even things you can do alone are better done with others. Whoever said "two heads are better than one" knew what they were talking about. Together, we can have a "good return" . . . better than by ourselves.

Take a look at Deuteronomy 32:30 and write your observations on the implications of Moses' words.

Moses puts forward the question, *"How could one chase a thousand, and two put ten thousand to flight, unless their Rock had sold them, and the Lord had given them up?"* It would seem that behind these words he is saying that in biblical math one plus one can equal so much more than two. Our impact together is multiplied rather than simply added and can be far greater together than it would be separately.

The church I serve with is a part of the Southern Baptist Convention (SBC). This grouping of churches is not a denomination in the traditional sense. There is no central authority or hierarchy of bishops who oversee a district of churches. Each church functions autonomously with its own individual governing structure. However, through the Convention these many individual churches link arms for the purpose of global outreach. The SBC's structure reflects the realization that so much more could be accomplished in world evangelization if we worked together and pooled our resources. While supporting a full-time missionary might be too much for one local church to fund, several churches cooperating together could send out workers. The "Cooperative Program" of the SBC serves as a tangible example of the effective synergy that can occur when believers work together.

> *We can have a far greater impact together than we could*
> *by ourselves.*

Two are better than one. Three or more working together is even better. We need each other's help! We can have a far greater impact together than we could by ourselves. Together, Solomon says, we have a *"good return"* for our labors.

DAY TWO

IN COMMUNITY WE HAVE A GREATER SPIRITUAL STABILITY

Two is a very important number to God. He created us with two eyes, two ears, two arms and hands, two legs and feet, and even two lungs. A person can survive with only one of these, but in each case it is better to have both functioning . . . it is how God designed us. We see better with two eyes. We hear more clearly with both ears functioning properly. When it comes to legs, we are steadier on both of them than with only one. Recently, this was driven home to me in a very practical way. My wife tore her meniscus—the cushion of cartilage behind the kneecap—and had to have it repaired. Actually, she ended up having to have a couple of surgeries. The injury and its associated pain made her unstable on her feet. During her recovery I often had to help her with everyday tasks like getting out of the car or navigating stairs. She simply didn't have the stability she enjoyed before. She is recovered now, but the process was a good reminder to us both to be grateful for what we have.

> *". . . woe to the one who falls when there is not another to lift him*
> *up." (Ecclesiastes 4:10)*

Look at Ecclesiastes 4:10 and identify which facet of life this second analogy connects to.

_____

_____

_____

_____

Solomon writes, *"For if either of them falls, the one will lift up his companion."* It would seem that this second illustration relates to traveling. From a spiritual perspective that makes sense. The Bible describes the Christian life as a "walk" . . . a journey. Solomon continues the analogy, *"But woe to the one who falls when there is not another to lift him up."* It is a reality that traveling can be treacherous . . . there are hazards along the way. The key question for each of us is this: when we trip, is someone there to catch us? In community, we have a greater spiritual stability.

Read Proverbs 17:17 and write down your thoughts on how this applies to the believer.

Going it alone can be dangerous. It really is notable how often Solomon mentions the importance of weaving our lives together with others. In Proverbs 17:17 he expressed it this way: *"A friend loves at all times, And a brother is born for adversity."* Do you have people like that in your life? You need them. True friends are there for us in hard times and not just in the fun times. Family, and our brethren in the family of God, are there for us at our most difficult moments.

From the outset God designed for us to have people in our lives. Read Genesis 2:18 and reflect on its message in its immediate context as well as how the principle applies more broadly to our lives as Christians.

One of the most amazing aspects of this statement is that it is made in the context of the garden of Eden before sin had stained anything. Even in that perfect environment, there was one component that God acknowledged was not good. *"Then the Lord God said, 'It is not good for the man to be alone; I will make him a helper suitable for him.'"* Obviously, the immediate application is that He is talking about marriage, but the principle applies far more broadly. It is God's will for most to marry, but it is His will for all to be in community with others whether married or not.

> A man without a companion is like a left hand without the right."
>
> —The Talmud

God made us to have others in our lives. In the Talmud, the Jewish collection of rabbinical wisdom, we read: "A man without a companion is like a left hand without the right." I can't imagine how difficult simple things like washing hands are with only one hand. Ellie

Currier is a friend who grew up in our church. I've known her all her life. While in college she was in a car accident and tragically lost her left arm. After the initial trauma of physical recovery, she had to begin the challenging task of relearning how to do basic tasks like personal hygiene and everyday activities with one arm instead of two. While obviously my point is that two arms are better than one, the real point here is community. For Ellie community became especially important. Certainly, the church community rallied around her and her family as she adjusted to her new normal, but it was more than that. She connected with others in the disabled community through a ministry called Joni and Friends. Finding others like herself not only gave her the comfort of not feeling alone, but she also found much practical help as well. Eventually she began to participate in mission work reaching out to disabled people in other cultures. Ellie found support in community, but also a new sense of purpose and opportunity to be used in the lives of others. God created us for community, and finding it adds so much fulfillment to our lives.

📖 Reflect on Proverbs 11:14 from the vantage point of the spiritual stability we find in community with other believers and write down your observations.

_____

_____

_____

Two legs give us stability. Solomon saw advice that way. He knew that we make better decisions when we draw on the wisdom of others. In this verse from Proverbs, he contrasts decisions made alone with those made in the strength and support of the advice available to us in the community of believers. With no guidance, people are far more likely to fall. But *"with many counselors there is victory."* That's something you always have in community.

I don't usually read ancient philosophers, but I came across a quote as I was researching this lesson that impacted me. The Roman philosopher Cicero wrote, *"Friendship improves happiness and abates misery, by the doubling of our joy and the dividing of our grief."* Think about that. Let me ask you a question. Do you have Christian friends you can rejoice with? Do you have Christian friends you can grieve with? Do you have people in your life who congratulate you when you accomplish something big, or who bring you a meal when you are sick? Are you part of a community where people who care about you give you a hug when you need it? All of these are found in community.

> *Friendship improves happiness and abates misery, by the doubling of our joy and the dividing of our grief."*
>
> —Cicero

Let me be clear, I'm talking about more than just church attendance. You can show up Sunday after Sunday. You can sing; you can give; you can listen to the sermon and leave, and never really get to know anyone. Real community is when we plug in and get to know others well enough to be comfortable sharing our struggles with them and are safe enough for them to be able to do the same. God created us for community. Together in community we have a greater spiritual impact—a good return for our labors. In community we have a greater spiritual stability. We have people in our lives who lift us up when we fall.

Day Three

In Community We Have a Greater Spiritual Passion

Solomon's third illustration is from the cold of winter. In verse 11 he says, *"Furthermore, if two lie down together they keep warm, but how can one be warm alone?"* Certainly, the principle mentioned here applies to the physical realm. We are warmer together than we are alone. But I want you to see that the same principle is true in the spiritual realm as well. The late Bill Bright, the founder of Campus Crusade for Christ (Cru), was one of the great spiritual influences in my life. I came to Christ through his organization and served on its staff for seven years. A principle he used to repeat often when talking about the importance of Christian fellowship was this: several logs burn brightly together, but if you take one and set it aside on the hearth, the fire quickly goes out. The same is true in our spiritual lives. If the flames of our spiritual passion have diminished, it could be that we aren't around other believers in a meaningful way nearly often enough. It is great to worship together in a large gathering, but I'm talking about more than that. We need relationship with others. We need people in our lives who challenge us . . . who hold us accountable. We need friends who know us and who spur us on in our faith.

When I served on Cru staff as the Campus Director at the University of Tennessee, I did a lot of ministry with athletes. Each year we took a group of students to a Christian outreach conference in Daytona Beach over spring break. One particular year I had two pitchers from the UT baseball team, a back-up quarterback from the football team, and several other collegiate athletes with me—guys one would expect to be full of confidence and willing to take risks. I suggested they join me in party-crashing for the purpose of talking with spring-breakers about Christ, and I was amazed at how timid they suddenly became. This was definitely something outside their comfort zone, and I am certain none of them would have done such a thing on their own. But they were willing to give it a shot if I took the lead. They were all braver as a group than they would have been alone. Afterward, as we debriefed, to a man they were all fired up about what had transpired, the open doors God had provided and the great conversations we were able to have about Christ in the most unlikely of circumstances. In community with each other, we gain fire from the logs around us and have a greater spiritual passion.

> *"As iron sharpens iron, so one man sharpens another."*
> (Proverbs 27:17)

📖 Reflect on Proverbs 27:17 and write your observations on its message to this subject of spiritual passion.

_____

_____

_____

_____

As I began to study this topic, I was amazed at how much Solomon wrote about the subject of community. This message from Proverbs 27:17 uses analogy to make a very important and relevant point. In the same way that *"Iron sharpens iron,"* the result of our interaction with each other is that *"one man sharpens another."* Even if there is friction, the net result is a sharper tool. Who are the spiritual sharpeners in your life? We find those people in the context of community.

How do the words of Hebrews 10:24 define community in a practical sense?

_____

_____

_____

_____

_____

This verse in the book of Hebrews gives us a good definition of biblical community. The first principle it speaks of is to *"consider."* This speaks of intentionality. Part of our benefit and responsibility in relationship with each other in the body of Christ is that we ought to intentionally be looking for ways to provoke, to stir up each other toward love and good deeds. Do you have people in your life who spur you on spiritually? That is one of the ways we rob ourselves when we isolate. It is also one of the ways we rob the fellowship of believers, since we are to be that catalyst for others as well.

Look at the next verse in that passage, Hebrews 10:25 and express in your own words what it has to say about the need to embrace community and reject isolation.

_____

_____

_____

_____

Having just encouraged us to stimulate each other toward love and good deeds, this next verse reminds us that in order for us to benefit from body life and for others to be blessed by our participation, we can't *"forsake"* assembling together with the church body, for it is when we are gathered with other believers in community that we are best positioned to encourage each other. Apparently, the author of Hebrews is concerned that some believers had left behind their previous habit of gathering regularly with other Christians. From the author's vantage point, the need to do so grows ever greater the closer we get to our Lord's return.

 DID YOU KNOW?
Synagogue

The Greek word translated *"assembling together"* in Hebrews 10:25 is the prefix *epi* (meaning "upon"), and the root word *sunagoge* (meaning "to gather together). It appears with the definite article and carries with it the meaning of "the assembly"—the Jewish equivalent of the New Testament church.

One of the biggest sins in churches today is that we don't assemble as consistently as we should—isolation sets in. According to Thom Ranier, "About 20 years ago, a church member was considered active in the church if he or she attended three times a week. Today, a church member is considered active if he or she attends three times a month. In many places it is even lower (https://www.christianitytoday.com/karl-vaters/2018/may/church-attendance-patterns-are-changing-we-have-to-adapt.html).

Sometimes missing is unavoidable because of work or illness. Often however, this inconsistency stems from a lack of priority. The closer we get to Christ's return, the more we need to assemble with other believers—the more we need Christian community, and that doesn't happen overnight. Meaningful interaction with others in the family of faith requires involvement and commitment. Floating church members make for a sinking church.

God created us for community. In community we have a greater spiritual impact (a better return for our labors). In community we have a greater spiritual stability (we are able to lift others up when they fall and have others to lift us up in our time of need). In community we have a greater spiritual passion (we are better positioned to warm each other spiritually).

Day Four

In Community We Have a Greater Spiritual Security

There is much to be learned from the animal kingdom that reflects the importance of community. For many practical reasons, fish swim in schools. There is greater safety in numbers. When a school of fish encounters a predator, not only are the odds of survival better for each individual if the group is attacked, but from a distance being compacted together gives the appearance of a much larger organism. If the school is attacked, it disperses and scrambles in multiple directions, making it more difficult for the forager to focus. Traveling together also increases the chances to find a mate. Geese fly as a group, in a "V" formation, for pragmatic reasons as well. Flying takes a lot of energy. The goose in the lead pushes the air to the side and leaves a sweet spot behind that other birds are able to take advantage of, expending less energy and thus being able to fly greater distances. When the lead bird gets tired, it drops back in the formation and another bird moves to the front. This formation also makes it easier for all the geese to maintain visual contact with each other, so they are oriented in the right direction and don't get lost. Wolves hunt in packs because together they are able to tackle much larger prey than they could hope to overpower on their own. They may chase their intended target over long distances with different wolves fulfilling different roles in the hunt according to size and ability. But part of the key to their success is to cull an individual animal such as a deer or elk away from the rest of the herd. Wolves are more formidable hunters because of community, and their prey are more vulnerable without it.

📖 Review Ecclesiastes 4:12 and answer the questions below.

According to verse 12, what are the benefits of community and the dangers of isolation?

_____

_____

_____

_____

Where do you think the principle of *"a cord of three strands"* fits in this equation?

_____

_____

_____

> *"And if one can overpower him who is alone, two can resist him. A cord of three strands is not quickly torn apart."* (Ecclesiastes 4:12)

In his fourth illustration, Solomon seems to draw his analogy from a military perspective. He makes the point that in community we have greater security, and in isolation we face greater danger. When we are alone, we can be overpowered by the enemy. The *"cord of three strands"* may be a reference to the larger community of believers, but it also may be an inference to the role the Lord plays in the process. Speaking of church discipline and its objective of restoring a sinning brother, Matthew 18:20 states, *". . . where two or three have gathered together in My name, I am there in their midst."* Performing such a difficult task as confronting sin is likely to be done more prudently and sensitively in the context of plurality, and there is security in weaving the Lord into the process.

What does Proverbs 15:22 indicate are the benefits of involving others in our decision-making?

_____

_____

_____

While at a glance one might not think of this verse from the vantage point of community, it serves as yet another example in Solomon's repertoire. He states that *"without consultation, plans are frustrated, but with many counselors they succeed."* We make better decisions with the input of others than we do on our own. One of the benefits of the body of Christ is that walking in relationship with our brothers and sisters in God's family affords us a broad diversity of expertise upon which we may draw. So which way do you live your Christian life?

📖 Read 2 Samuel 11:1–4 and reflect how the danger of isolation may have contributed to David's stumbling.

_____

_____

_____

_____

In this tragic narrative from the life of King David we see the inherent danger of isolation. At a time when he typically would have gone to war with his "mighty men," he chose to take a vacation. Alone, separated from the accountability and encouragement of his brethren, he succumbed to temptation and stumbled terribly. This "man after God's own heart" committed adultery as well as murder in his attempted cover-up once Bathsheba became pregnant. There were far-reaching consequences to David's sin, and God records the process of his stumbling to underscore for all that when we are isolated, we can more easily fall prey to temptation. The greatest sins of David's life happened when he went solo.

The greatest sins of David's life happened when he went solo.

📖 Consider John 20:24-25 and answer the questions that follow.

Verse 25 gives John's account of Thomas after the crucifixion. Why is he called "doubting Thomas"?

_____

Looking at verse 24, what contributed to his doubting?

_____

_____

_____

Most of us have heard of "doubting Thomas." In John 20:25 we see the statement that earned him that nickname. When the other disciples related to him about seeing the resurrected Lord, he refused to believe. In this verse he states, *"Unless I see in His hands the imprint of the nails, and put my finger into the place of the nails, and put my hand into His side, I will not believe."* So why did he doubt? Verse 24 indicates he doubted because he wasn't with the others when they saw the Lord. He had isolated himself. He wasn't in the Upper Room when Jesus showed up. It is easy to doubt by yourself, and you can't easily answer your own questions. This is another reason why we need each other—we need each other's help in times of struggle.

📖 Consider Hebrews 3:13 and write your observations on our need for one another and what can happen in isolation.

_____

_____

_____

_____

Isolation not only robs us of the help of others, it makes us inconsequential in the lives of others. Hebrews 3:13 says, *"But encourage one another day after day as long as it is still called today."* Every day is an opportunity to encourage others and be encouraged by others. Once the day is done, that chance has passed. The consequence of not doing so is the potential that we or others might be *"hardened by the deceitfulness of sin."*

When we isolate from others we can't be there to help when they need it. Maybe you are thinking, "I have my spouse." That is great if you are so blessed, but that one relationship can't meet all your needs. It isn't supposed to. But what about those who are single? Community is about more than your spouse or family. Biblical community is about the entire family of God.

> *"But encourage one another day after day as long as it is still called 'today,' so that none of you will be hardened by the deceitfulness of sin." (Hebrews 3:13)*

Day Five

For Me to Follow God

Why do we isolate ourselves as Christians? This is an important question to grapple with as we seek to apply this week's study. Sometimes we isolate to *insulate* . . . to protect ourselves. Perhaps the driving motivation is fear, shaped by insecurities and negative experiences from our upbringing. Maybe we go it alone because we are avoiding past pain. It is possible that we isolate ourselves because we are uncomfortable being vulnerable with people who know our junk. Sometimes isolation stems from avoiding conflict and confrontation. Some of us do it to punish others who've hurt us. One reason for isolation and avoiding community is as a consequence of sin—both specific sins and our general sin nature. Sin always creates distance between us and God and between us and each other. From the very beginning, going all the way back to Genesis 3 and the failure of Adam and Eve in the garden, sin has caused us to hide from each other and from God. Another reason for isolation is simply a choice of our pride and flesh. Perhaps we don't want to be accountable for our actions. Pride whispers the lie that we don't need help . . . that we can handle things on our own. Has your own sin isolated you?

We all likely remember the story Jesus taught in Luke 15 known as the "parable of the Prodigal Son." The prodigal wanted to enjoy his inheritance without having to wait for it. When it was given by his father, he left his community behind, and with it, the accountability, encouragement, and support he had long taken for granted. When he had squandered away his resources, hard times fell, and he found himself alone and unvalued, working in a pig sty with less to eat than the pigs. He only found restoration and redemption when he returned to his father and the community that cared about him. One of the most important realities in a person's life is who you do life with. Perhaps the greatest social epidemic of our time is loneliness. It is a crucial issue in modern culture with enormous consequences.

If technologies take the place of face-to-face, heart-to-heart,
human interaction, we have traded real community for a façade,
and something deep in our souls begins to suffer.

Recently I came across an article that first appeared in *USA Today* in May 2018. The author related that loneliness and isolation don't just make us sad—they can literally make us sick. Drawing on research funded by Cigna, a leading U.S. health insurance provider, the article reports that loneliness actually has the same effect on mortality as smoking fifteen cigarettes a day and is even more dangerous to societal health than obesity. The article went on to say that "face-to-face conversation is the antidote." Many today spend their spare time at home, alone. They eat alone. Perhaps they watch television or play video games by themselves. Far too many people feel alienated, lonely, and depressed. The hectic pace of life so encroaches that we don't think we have enough time for relationships and for spending time with others in community. I find it ironic that in this day of social media, we are becoming less social than ever. Social media creates an artificial sense of omnipresence—enabling us to virtually connect so many other places that it can have the unintended result of keeping us from truly engaging where we are. Texting, emailing, and social networking through mediums like Facebook or Instagram aren't bad habits in themselves, but genuine human interaction cannot be replaced by modern technology. They can help us be aware of what is going on in the lives of others as part of our interaction with them. But if they take the place of face-to-face, heart-to-heart, human interaction, we have traded real community for a façade, and something deep in our souls begins to suffer.

Identify the dominant technologies that tend to absorb your time (rank in order of prominence):

___ talking on a cell phone

___ texting

___ iPad® or tablet use

___ Internet research

___ email

___ watching programs via television or streaming on other devices

___ listening to podcasts or music

___ games (on your phone or playing video games)

On the scale below, indicate the overall impact technology has had on your relationships?

NEGATIVE ◁ 1 —— 2 —— 3 —— 4 —— 5 —— 6 —— 7 ▷ POSITIVE

How much time would you say you spend with technology each week? . . . with interpersonal social interaction?

_____

_____

_____

What changes in this area do you feel are warranted based on our study in Lesson One?

_____

_____

_____

God wants community for us, and for that to be a reality we need to make the time. The Bible is clear: If we want to experience God's presence, we are to seek Him through His word and surrender to His Holy Spirit, and also through relationships with other people.

> *"Day by day continuing with one mind in the temple, and breaking*
> *bread from house to house, they were taking their meals together*
> *with gladness and sincerity of heart." (Acts 2:46)*

📖 Take a few moments to reflect on Acts 2:42–47.

What priority did the first century church place on Christian fellowship?

_____

_____

_____

What did that look like practically?

_____

_____

_____

What resulted from their emphasis on community?

_____

_____

_____

Acts 2:42 says that for the first century church, only the Word of God was a higher priority than fellowship. Verse 44 says they were *"together."* One should be wary of reading too much into this, but apparently one of the results of their godly priorities is that *they wanted* to be together. They did life together. We see from this passage that their church involvement included large group gatherings (v.46—*"continuing with one mind in the temple"*) but also small-group get-togethers (*"breaking bread from house to house, they were taking their meals together with gladness and sincerity of heart"*). One of the results was unity (*"with one mind"*), but as verse 47 points out, another practical result was people being saved. Nothing sets the church apart from the world like authentic community.

More often than not, the way you'll tangibly feel God's love and His presence is from the people who have him living inside—the people that love Him. He isn't typically going to show up in some visible, mystical form. He's going to show up in a friend—a brother or sister in Christ. The Bible makes it clear that we are the *body* of Christ, the family of God.

What can you do about isolation? You don't need to go through life as Lone Rangers—we should be like the "Power Rangers®," doing everything as part of a team with people who have our backs.

Why not start now by establishing some new habits. Prayerfully consider the list below and check any action points that apply to you personally...

___ Commit to investigate a Sunday school class or Sunday morning group at your church—a place where you can build community and do life together with others for mutual encouragement.

___ Join a small group Bible study in your neighborhood (it doesn't have to be on a Sunday morning)

___ Start a small-group Bible study at your home or work.

___ Ask someone to join you for lunch or for dinner. Even when you are busy, you are still going to eat, so this is a way to double up your time.

___ Engage: Volunteer for something new and serve with a team of others you can get to know and build community with.

___ Do hobbies together with other Christians (sports, crafts, etc.). However, if you do, don't leave out the spiritual dimension. Take time for everyone to share what is going on in their lives and pray for each other.

Most of the things we are doing now, can be done with others without adding any time to our busy schedules . . . it just requires making community a priority. As you close this week's lesson, write out a prayer to the Lord that reflects your heart on this issue of community.

NOTES

LESSON 2

LOVING ONE ANOTHER

We live in a world of commandments—rules of what we can and cannot do. At a glance, faith may seem to be maintaining a set of rules. After all, didn't God give Moses a top ten list during his forty days on Mount Sinai? In fact, those Ten Commandments were written in stone and carried with Israel wherever they went. Rabbis and theologians continued to refine and redefine the rules throughout the years. What began as ten commands had been expanded into a massive rule book with 613 commands by the time of Jesus' earthly ministry.

Faith had become so complicated and confusing that only the professionals could live it. God's guidance for life had become a weighty burden. If this were the way faith was supposed to be lived, one would expect Jesus to applaud it. Instead of complimenting the Pharisees, however, Jesus condemned them as hypocrites. In Matthew 15:7-9 Jesus called their faith *"vain worship"* because they had turned their own ideas into doctrine. They had become so adept at keeping rules that they were not aware that they had distanced themselves from God. They lost the point that the ultimate objective of every commandment was relationship. The reason we repent of idolatry and Sabbath breaking and taking the Lord's name in vain is for the sake of relationship with God. The reason we repent of stealing and adultery and murder is for the sake of relationship with our fellow man.

". . . You shall love your neighbor as yourself" (Matthew 22:39)

One day a lawyer posed a question to Jesus—not a courtroom lawyer like we think of today, but an expert in Mosaic law. He was a legalist—a "theological nitpicker." Most likely he had already decided which commandment was the greatest and wanted to see if Jesus agreed with him. Christ's answer had to be unexpected. Quoting from Deuteronomy 6:5, Jesus replies, *"You shall love the Lord your God with all your heart, and with all your soul, and with all your mind"* (Matthew 22:37). Not only does He give an authoritative response, calling it *"the greatest and foremost commandment,"* He also answers the unasked question of which is number two on the list. Referencing Leviticus 19:18, He adds, *". . . You shall love your neighbor as yourself"* (Matthew 22:39). Christ makes it clear that every other biblical directive was given to enable us to live out these two relationship mandates. This value is easily seen in the Ten Commandments, as the first four directly deal with our relationship with God, and the remaining six deal with our relationships with other people.

Day One

Love, the Final Apologetic

Liza was suffering from a rare and serious disease. Her only chance of recovery appeared to be a blood transfusion from her five-year-old brother, who miraculously survived the same disease and had developed the antibodies needed to combat the illness. The doctor explained the situation to her little brother and asked the boy if he would be willing to give his blood for his sister. He hesitated for a moment and said, "Yes, I'll do it if it will save Liza." As the transfusion progressed, he lay in bed next to his sister and smiled, seeing the color return to her cheeks. Then his face grew pale, and his smile faded. He looked up at the doctor and asked with a trembling voice, "Will I start to die right away?" Being young, the boy had misunderstood the doctor. He thought he was going to have to give her all his blood. The little boy had been willing to give his life for his sister's need. That kind of love that puts others before self is what it means to love one another as Christ loved us. That is sincere love. That is fervent love.[1]

📖 Read John 13:34.

What does Jesus mean by calling this a "new commandment"?

_____

_____

What is the context of this statement, and how does this affect our view of Jesus' words?

_____

_____

_____

"A new commandment I give to you, that you love one another,
even as I have loved you, that you also love one another"
(John 13:34)

📖 Examine John 15:12, 17, and 17:26. What do these add to our understanding of Jesus' command?

_____

_____

_____

To address the wrong perspective that had developed in Judaism, Jesus adds a new item to the Ten Commandments His disciples had been taught: *"A new commandment I give to you, that you love one another, even as I have loved you, that you also love one another"* (John 13:34). We are commanded to love one another with the same kind of committed, unconditional love that God shows us. At the beginning of the "Upper Room Discourse," Jesus uttered this "New Commandment." Jesus knew this conversation would be His last with the twelve before He would be crucified. Obviously, this gives even greater weight to His words. Before the night was over, He repeated it twice more: *"This is My commandment, that you love one another, just as I have loved you"* (John 15:12). *"This I command you, that you love one another"* (John 15:17). I think He wanted to make sure they got the point. It is significant and noteworthy that this desire appears in the last words Jesus prayed before He was arrested in Gethsemane: *". . . that the love with which You the Father loved Me may be in them, and I in them"* (John 17:26). Jesus prays that all who believe would love one another.

📖 Take a look at John 13:35 and write your observations on the implications of that statement.

....

....

....

....

It will be obvious to everyone that we follow Christ . . . not by showing love to Him, but if we *"have love for one another."* The great Christian philosopher Francis Schaeffer called love "the final apologetic"—the ultimate proof of our faith. By the presence of true, unconditional love in our lives, the unbelieving world can recognize the difference following Jesus makes.

The word "love" is used in a thousand different ways. We *love* apple pie, baseball, tennis, mom, and God. We use one word—love—to describe how we feel toward something or someone, but love is much more than that one word, and it is certainly more than a feeling that you feel when you feel that way. What does it mean to love one another? We know that this is important to Jesus because He gave this as the new commandment—not new because it had never been commanded before, because Leviticus talks about loving one's neighbor. This new command would be fulfilled with a new power—His Spirit within each heart. We know this command is important to the Father because His children would be *"taught by God to love one another"* (1 Thessalonians. 4:9). What does it mean then?

> The great Christian philosopher Francis Schaeffer called love "the
> final apologetic"—the ultimate proof of our faith.

Loving one another will mean being real, giving unselfishly, and going the extra mile with someone or for someone. It will mean relying on the power of the Spirit—not the pulse of our feelings. It is a choice—sometimes it feels good, sometimes it doesn't. Sometimes it's tough and takes a lot of energy, but we go ahead because it's the right thing to do.

DAY TWO

A DEBT OF LOVE

How much debt do you carry? A little? A lot? None? The total American consumer debt (excluding mortgages and car loans) first topped $1 trillion in 1994. It has more than doubled since then. The average household has about $12,000 in this kind of debt.[2] The bottom line is that we owe a lot! Is this wrong? Some take Paul's words in Romans 13:8:"*Owe nothing to anyone except to love one another*" to mean that a Christian should never have any debt under any circumstances. Actually, the word *owe* is in the present tense. The implication is that we should not *keep* owing someone a debt. In other words, if we have a debt, we should pay it off. The balance should diminish. In truth, the point here isn't about finances at all—it is about love.

📖 Read Romans 13:8 and write down your thoughts on how this applies to the believer.

Do you count love among your obligations? Paul is saying that this is the only kind of obligation whose balance doesn't diminish with each payment. Love is the permanent debt. There is a point of clarity we must not miss in Paul's words. When he speaks of love, he isn't just talking about how you feel toward others. Both uses of the word *love* in this verse are verbs—actions—not nouns. In other words, they are what we do, not what we possess.

📖 What point is Jesus making in Luke 6:32 about how we are to love?

Most think we have accomplished something worthy and laudable when we show love to others. We deserve a pat on the back, and if our deeds are especially benevolent, a trophy is in order. Not so, says Jesus. When we show love, we haven't done the extraordinary. We are merely making payments on a debt we owe. The Pharisees taught to love your neighbor and hate your enemies. Jesus challenged this notion: "*and if you love those who love you, what credit is that to you? For even sinners love those who love them*" (Luke 6:32). God wants His people to be a community known by love—a commitment to love by choice, not feelings.

How does the example of God the Father in Luke 6:35 speak to how we tend to love?

_____

_____

_____

> "Love is patient, love is kind and is not jealous, love does not brag
> and is not arrogant, love does not act unbecomingly, it does not
> seek its own, is not provoked, does not take into account a wrong
> suffered, does not rejoice in unrighteousness, but rejoices with the
> truth; bears all things, believes all things, hopes all things, endures
> all things. Love never fails." (1 Corinthians 13:4–8a)

Speaking of God, Jesus adds in Luke 6:35, "*. . . for He Himself is kind to ungrateful and evil men.*" We only applaud ourselves for acts of love because we compare ourselves to each other. None of us consistently loves as God does.

DAY THREE

THE SOURCE OF LOVE

A friend was in a tight spot. His marriage was on the rocks. As a last-ditch hope, he agreed to counseling. The counselor asked, "Do you love your wife?" "What?" he exclaimed, "of course I love my wife!" The counselor began to read Paul's description of love from the Bible, "*Love is patient, love is kind and is not jealous, love does not brag and is not arrogant, love does not act unbecomingly, it does not seek its own, is not provoked, does not take into account a wrong suffered, does not rejoice in unrighteousness, but rejoices with the truth; bears all things, believes all things, hopes all things, endures all things. Love never fails.*" "Do you love your wife?" he asked again. My friend hung his head and honestly admitted, "No." It was a hard pill to swallow, but truth helped him see that in both attitude and action he wasn't really loving her. That was a step in the right direction, but even more important was his realization that he didn't know God. You see, we cannot love others the way God wants without first experiencing His love for us. "*. . . the fruit of the Spirit is love*" (Galatians 5:22). It is God who enables us to pay our debt of love.

📖 Reflect on 1 John 4:7 and make note of your observations on what this verse teaches.

_____

_____

_____

We are supposed to love one another. We know that. But where does this love come from? Must we grit our teeth and try to make it happen? It is clear from John's words that being *born of God* is essential. Apart from being spiritually reborn, we are not capable of loving others with this kind of love. But John doesn't stop there. He also includes that one *knows God* as an enabling credential. While the two may appear as synonyms, the text clearly separates them. The word *born* in the original Greek is in the perfect tense. This means it is a completed act. The word *knows* is in the present tense and indicates an ongoing action. We must be a Christian to love as God loves, but we must also grow.

> *Apart from being spiritually reborn, we are not capable of loving*
> *others with this kind of love.*

📖 How do John's words in 1 John 4:8 and 4:19 speak to the source of Christian love?

We get to know God by spending time with Him, by obeying what He says, and by dealing with wrongs as He convicts us. The longer we pursue this relationship, the more we become like Him—the One who loves. John continues the thought he began in 4:7 with verse 8, telling us, *"The one who does not love does not know God, for God is love."* If we are really going to love one another, we need to spend time with God who *"is love."* John tells us that *"We love, because He first loved us"* (1 John 4:19).

📖 Review 1 John 4:9–11 and answer the questions below.

According to verse 9, what does this kind of love looks like?

What does verse 10 add to our understanding of God's love?

How should we respond to being loved by God based on verse 11?

What does this kind of love look like? First John 4:9 tells us, *"By this the love of God was manifested in us, that God has sent His only begotten Son into the world so that we might live through Him."* God loved us by giving of Himself sacrificially to meet our needs. Again, this is more than just an example to follow; it is an enablement. Verse 10 continues, *"In this is love, not that we loved God, but that He loved us and sent His Son to be the propitiation for our sins."* God took the initiative. He *"loved"* us. He showed us grace. He didn't love us because we deserved it. He didn't love us because of anything we did. He simply *chose* to love us. All of this leads us to 1 John 4:11: *"Beloved, if God so loved us, we also ought to love one another."* We are supposed to love one another, but not merely in the natural, human way. The natural way to love others is conditional love—"I love you because . . ." or "I love you if . . . ." As Christians, if we only love conditionally, we are no different than the world. God wants us to love others because of *Him*, not because of *them*. He wants us to love unconditionally.

> The natural way to love others is conditional love: "I love you because . . ." or "I love you if. . . ." As Christians, if we only love conditionally, we are no different than the world.

The subject of love was so important to John because he was gripped by the love of God. In his gospel, he repeatedly identifies himself as *"the disciple whom Jesus loved"* (Jn. 13:23; 19:26; 20:2; 21:7; 21:20). He uses the word *love* 109 times in his gospel and epistles. Love mattered to him because this former "son of thunder" had experienced being loved with God's love. We must draw on God's love to be able to love one another as we should. When we do, we help enable others to love. John closes out this thought in 1 John 4:12, saying, *"No one has seen God at any time; if we love one another, God abides in us, and His love is perfected in us."* Although no one has seen God, they can see Him in us if we love one another.

DAY FOUR

LOVING BY PUTTING OTHERS FIRST

On December 4, 2006, manning a .50-caliber machine gun in the turret of a Humvee in Iraq, Pfc. Ross McGinnis could see the insurgent fling a hand grenade at his vehicle from a rooftop. He shouted and tried to deflect it, but it fell inside near four of his buddies. What followed was a stunning act of self-sacrifice. McGinnis, a 19-year-old from rural Pennsylvania and the youngest soldier in his unit, threw himself backward onto the grenade, absorbing the blast with his body. He was killed instantly. The others escaped serious injury.[3] Private McGinnis was posthumously awarded the Medal of Honor, and rightly so. We hold such sacrifice in awe. He literally laid down his life for his friends.

Ross McGinnis' example extends far beyond his one final act of self-sacrifice. In a statement released by his parents, we are told: "Ross did not become OUR hero by dying to save his fellow soldiers from a grenade. He was a hero to us long before he died, because he was willing to risk his life to protect the ideals of freedom and justice that America represents. . . . The lives of four men who were his Army brothers outweighed the value of his one life. It was just a matter of simple kindergarten arithmetic. Four means more than one. It didn't matter to Ross that he could have escaped the situation without a scratch. Nobody would have questioned such a reflex reaction. What mattered to him were the four men placed in his care on a moment's notice. One moment he was responsible for defending the rear of the convoy from enemy fire; the next moment he held the lives of four of his friends in his hands."[4] He was already living a life of putting the welfare and safety of others ahead of his own. It was his lifestyle of laying down himself for others that made the decision of an instant his natural reflex. Were he accustomed to living selfishly, he would have reacted differently.

What does John 15:12–13 indicate it looks like to love one another as He loved us?

_____

_____

_____

> *As difficult as it would be for any of us to make that huge choice of*
> *a moment to sacrifice our lives to save others, in some ways*
> *it is even more difficult to make the little choices every day to put*
> *others first.*

In John 15:12, Jesus told His disciples, *"This is My commandment, that you love one another, just as I have loved you."* He followed this up by clarifying that the greatest act of love one could do was to lay down his or her life for others.

As difficult as it would be for any of us to make that huge choice of a moment to sacrifice our lives to save others, in some ways it is even more difficult to make the little choices every day to put others first. Those are not dramatic, life-or-death decisions. Yet they shape the measure of our character. Jesus commanded us to love one another. In this same conversation, He said, *"You did not choose Me but I chose you, and appointed you that you would go and bear fruit, and that your fruit would remain, so that whatever you ask of the Father in My name He may give to you"* (John 15:16). What kind of fruit does Christ want us to bear? *"This I command you, that you love one another"* (John 15:17).

What is your attitude toward others in the church? Does it reflect the humble mindset which sees others as more important, or does your attitude communicate that you are the most important person in each relationship? Notice, I am not asking about your actions—how you treat others. I am talking about your attitude—what you think in your heart about others. As Christians, we probably are conditioned to *say* that others are more important, but that only lasts until our rights are infringed upon. Then our attitude reveals itself. Chuck Swindoll has this to say about "attitude": "The longer I live the more convinced I become that life is 10 percent what happens to us and 90 percent how we respond to it."[5] That's a pretty clear statement about the importance of our attitude.

📖 Read Philippians 2:3–4 and reflect on the questions below.

Thinking about the context from which Paul shares these words—wrongful imprisonment in Rome—how does Paul's attitude look differently than one might expect?

_____

_____

_____

Make a list of the terms in these verses and reflect on what the opposite of Paul's exhortation would be.

_____

_____

_____

_____

When Paul wrote Philippians 2, he had plenty of opportunity to have a bad attitude. He was imprisoned in Rome because of the lies of his enemies, yet his attitude was sterling—he had no complaints. The Lord was with him in his prison cell, and he ministered to soldiers and to the many, many visitors who came to see him and to listen to him teach and preach about Jesus and the kingdom of God (Acts 28:30–31). He was living out what he wrote to the Romans: "*Be devoted to one another in brotherly love; give preference to one another in honor*" (Romans 12:10).

> "Have this attitude in yourselves which was also in Christ Jesus."
> (Philippians 2:5)

What does Paul set in Philippians 2:5 as the standard of what our attitude ought to be?

_____

_____

_____

In those dark circumstances, Paul experienced the encouragement of Christ and the love and fellowship of the Spirit (2:1). There he discovered the joy of humility—of what it means to regard others as more important—and of serving others' interests and not just his own (2:3). When he thought about the matter of mindset or attitude, he thought of Christ whose heart and mindset were perfect. Christ was willing to take the form of a bondservant to serve others even to the point of death on a Roman cross. He gave His life serving His Father and us.

Compare Philippians 1:21 with Philippians 2:1–2 and identify what you can of the source and nature of Paul's attitude.

_____

_____

_____

_____

When Christ is our Life (as He was for Paul—Philippians 1:21), and when we are walking surrendered to Him, we will experience that same encouragement and love of Christ as well as the fellowship of the Spirit that Paul mentions in Philippians 2:1. These are the basis of a right relationship with others that he begins talking about in verse 2—a relationship marked by oneness of mind and heart, by *agapē* love, by a unity of spirit and a oneness of purpose (everyone has the same goal). That is also the basis of *a right attitude toward one another*—verses 3 and 4. When Christ is our Life, people are not a problem. They are our opportunity to express humility, genuine love, and a servant's heart in looking out for their needs. Paul goes on to talk about two men who showed this same kind of attitude. Not only do we see it in Christ, we see it in Timothy and Epaphroditus (2:19–30).

DAY FIVE

FOR ME TO FOLLOW GOD

In his first epistle, Peter teaches that one of the consequences of having *purified* our souls by obedience to the truth is to the end that we have "*a sincere love of the brethren*" (1 Peter 1:22). The word *sincere* means a love that is not hypocritical or two-faced. Doesn't it break your heart when someone is two-faced? Paul exhorted in Romans 12:9, "*let love be without hypocrisy.*" True love is always sincere, with no mixed motives. Peter states that our love should be *fervent.* The Greek word not only has the idea of intensity, but also of intentionality. Fervent love doesn't happen by accident and is not driven merely by feelings. The root idea is one stretching forward with all one's might like a runner at the finish line of a race. The clear message of Peter is that loving the brethren is not something we do whenever we get around to it; we must purpose to love. This idea of intentionality is echoed by the author of Hebrews: "*. . . let us consider how to stimulate one another to love and good deeds.*" We should not only love each other, but we should devise ways to motivate each other toward love. Peter considers this message of fervency so important that he repeats it: "*Above all, keep fervent in your love for one another, because love covers a multitude of sins*" (1 Peter 4:8). When we are making the effort to love others, we make it easier for our own faults to be overlooked.

> "*Above all, keep fervent in your love for one another, because love covers a multitude of sins*" (1 Peter 4:8)

How, based on your experience, do you think the followers of Christ are doing at loving one another as Christ loved?

_____

_____

_____

_____

What would people say about Christ and about your faith if they could see your attitude toward others in your life?

_____

_____

_____

We have seen Christ repeatedly command us to love one another. We have seen Paul repeat this idea again and again in his epistles. (To the Corinthians: "*Let all that you do be done in love*" [1 Cor. 16:14]; To the Colossians: "*beyond all these things put on love, which is the perfect bond of unity*" [Col. 3:14]). We have seen multiple exhortations to love from John, the disciple whom Jesus loved. Here we see Peter repeatedly calling us to fervently love one another. Why all this concern? The context of Peter's call in 4:8 to "*keep fervent in your love for one another*" is his reminder in 1 Peter 4:7, "*The end of all things is near.*" Consider the following verses. Speaking of the end times, Jesus said, "*Because lawlessness is increased, most people's love will grow cold*" (Matthew 24:12). Paul warned that in the last days, "*. . . men will be lovers of self, lovers of money . . . lovers of pleasure rather than lovers of God*" (2 Timothy 3:2–4). The world has become a very selfish place. Unfortunately, Paul goes on to point out in the next verse that these are not people outside the church. These selfish people may not be Christians, but they are "*holding to a form of godliness*" (2 Timothy 3:5). The closer we get to Christ's return, the *more* we need to be fervent about loving one another.

Before this lesson, did you view love as doing something good or as a debt to be paid? Place an X on the scale below to represent your views before the lesson and circle where you would place yourself now.

LOVE IS A
GOOD   1   2   3   4   5   6   7   DEBT
DEED   OWED

Do you view love as doing something good or as a debt to be paid?

Are you drawing on God's love to be able to love others as you should?

_____

_____

_____

_____

One of the ways we draw on God's love is by spending time with Him. When we talk with God, what should we speak about? I have always found the "ACTS" acrostic as a good guide for prayer. In this system, the letters "A-C-T-S" stand for adoration, confession, thanksgiving and supplication. All are types of prayer admonished in Scripture, but I think this order is important. By beginning with adoration—we start with our eyes on God instead of ourselves. Confession should naturally flow out of focusing on who God is. With our eyes on Him, we will be sensitive to anything that stands between us and Him. Thanksgiving should come before supplication. We should be mindful of what God has already done before requesting what we would like to see Him do. I offer this as a general guideline for talking with God.

As you close out this week's lesson, express your heart and what you have learned in some written prayers...

_____

_____

_____

_____

_____

_____

_____

_____

_____

_____

Works Cited

1. Jack Canfield and Mark Victor Hansen, *Chicken Soup for the Soul* (Deerfield Beach, FL: Health Communications, 1993), pp.27–28.

2. http://www.creditcards.com/credit-card-industry-facts-and-personal-debt-statistics.php

3. http://www.washingtonpost.com/wp-dyn/content/article/2007/01/01/AR2007010100759.html

4. http://www.washingtonpost.com/wp-dyn/content/article/2007/01/01/AR2007010100760.html

5. Charles Swindoll, *The Grace Awakening* (Nashville, TN: Thomas Nelson Publishers, 2003).

NOTES

LESSON 3

MINISTERING TO ONE ANOTHER

The year was 1940. The French army, the pride of Europe, had just collapsed under the siege of Hitler's "blitzkrieg." The Dutch had been overwhelmed. The Belgians had surrendered. The British army, briefly trapped, fought free and retreated to a tiny fishing town on the coast of France—the channel port of Dunkirk (then spelled Dunkerque). Their faces were turned to the might of Hitler's Third Reich, and their backs were to the sea. In the words of William Manchester, "It was England's greatest crises since the Norman conquest . . . This time Britain stood alone." Two hundred and twenty thousand of Britain's finest young men seemed doomed to die. The Fuhrer's troops, only miles away in the hills of France, didn't realize how close to victory they actually were. Any rescue attempt seemed feeble and futile in the time remaining. A thin British navy, "the professionals," told King George VI that they would be lucky to save seventeen thousand troops—less than ten percent of the men. The House of Commons was warned to prepare for "hard and heavy tidings." Politicians were paralyzed, the king was powerless, and the Americans could only watch as spectators from a distance. Then, as the doom of the British army seemed imminent, a strange fleet appeared on the horizon of the English Channel: the wildest assortment of boats perhaps ever assembled in history. Trawlers and tugs, scows and fishing sloops, lifeboats and pleasure craft, smacks and coasters, sailboats, an island ferry by the name of *Gracie Fields*, even *Endeavor*, Tom Sopwith's America's Cup challenger came, and the London fire brigade's fire-boat *Massey Shaw*. Each ship was manned by civilian volunteers—English fathers sailing to rescue Britain's exhausted bleeding sons. The drama was cinema-worthy as the award-winning 2017 Hollywood blockbuster, *Dunkirk*, attests. Manchester writes in the first installment of his epic biography of Winston Churchill, *The Last Lion*, that even today what happened in 1940 in less than 24 hours seems like a miracle—not only were all of the British soldiers rescued but numerous allied troops as well. Well over three hundred thousand troops were redeemed that day.

> *Today, the vast majority of Christians do not have any kind of personal ministry. Most have no idea what their spiritual gift is.*

The parallel today is striking. For too long the paid professionals (ministers, missionaries, and full-time Christian workers) have carried the load of the work of God in ministry, but that is not God's design. The needs of the world are too great to be met by so few. Even the needs of a church are too great to be effectively met by the paid professionals. Everyone's efforts are needed if the work of God is to be done. Each of us must make our contribution not just in finances, but in offering our own giftedness to minister to one another. That is the only way God's will is going to be done on earth. A church whose only ministry is done by the pastor will be a church doing very little for God's kingdom. God's design is for pastors to equip laypersons so *they*, the laity, can do the work of service.

But there is a problem. Today, the vast majority of Christians do not have any kind of personal ministry. Most have no idea what their spiritual gift is. According to a recent survey by the George Barna research organization, only about one fifth of churchgoers can identify a spiritual gift they think they possess. Equally disturbing from this research is the news that about one third of that number incorrectly identified theirs as something other than those Scripture lists as spiritual gifts. Even more startling is the reality that a great many Christians don't see any problem with that state of affairs because they think ministry is for the elite—the special people of the kingdom. They think they are supposed to be spectators. But if that were true, why did God give each one of us a spiritual gift? Why did Scripture instruct us to employ that gift for the common good? Sadly, many think they have a spiritual gift for their own personal use and edification. But that contradicts the clear teaching of each passage that gifts are ours for the sake of others. God wants us to minister to one another. He has made each Christian a minister! The work He wants done cannot be accomplished without all of us participating.

> *God wants us to minister to one another. He has made each*
> *Christian a minister!*

DAY 1

MINISTER TO ONE ANOTHER WITH OUR GIFTS (JOHN 13:34)

What do you expect of a "gifted" person? In our culture, a "gifted" athlete or musician is applauded and admired. A "gifted" leader usually is rewarded handsomely by his employer. When we encounter the "gifted," we expect them to be given prominence, and often they expect that as well. You can understand how the non-Christian would think that. If one does not believe in God and believes that we are all products of a Darwinian evolutionary process, then all accomplishments are attained by personal merit. We may use the term "gifted," but we really mean "earned." This "survival of the fittest" mentality champions the victor and forgets the vanquished. When we understand that we are not self-made, but have been created by God, everything appears in a different light. Our areas of giftedness must be recognized as just that—gifts. Years ago, someone shared with me that they had been blessed by my teaching. They asked, "What is the secret to how much more you get when you study than I do? Are you just a really diligent student?" As I reflected on the questions, in honesty I had to humbly confess, "No, I'm really not what you would call diligent." My teaching was my greatest contribution to them, and if God had "gifted" me, I couldn't even take credit for it. I had to recognize that whatever I had to offer another was because of Him, not me.

We must recognize the purpose for which our gifts were given. God wants us as His body to use our gifts and talents for the common good instead of living selfishly. We were never intended to be the sole beneficiaries of our giftedness. God blessed us with whatever talents we have—whether our abilities are athletic, musical, geared to public speaking, rooted in intelligence or business savviness—and He did so in order to make us a blessing to others. God desires that every believer be a minister, and not just a ministry. Not all of us will preach sermons or serve in vocational ministry, but each of us can be used of God to minister to someone else. If we have truly been born again, we have each been endowed with spiritual gifts. They were not given to us so that we could feel good about ourselves, but as Paul explained in 1 Corinthians 12:7, *"But to each one is given the manifestation of the Spirit for the common good."* In other words, the body of Christ should benefit because of our presence. God gives each of us gifts, and He gives each of us opportunities to exercise those gifts within the body of Christ "for the common good" so that the whole body is benefited. We are called to minister to one another.

What is your attitude about your gifts and talents? Do you give yourself credit and pat yourself on the back for them, or do you give God glory and recognize Him as the source of any good in you? A right thinking about your gifts and talents ought to produce an attitude of humility and of gratefulness to God as the author of them.

> *"As each one has received a special gift, employ it in serving*
> *one another as good stewards of the manifold grace of God."*
> (1 Peter 4:10)

📖 Read 1 Peter 4:10 and answer the questions that follow.

What is Peter's assumption here?

_____

_____

_____

_____

What are we to do with our giftedness?

_____

_____

_____

_____

_____

Peter begins these verses with an assumption—"*each one has received a special gift.*" He is speaking, of course, of what the Bible calls spiritual gifts. Everyone has at least one. That means we all have some kind of ministry to contribute. Since none of us possesses all the gifts, it is guaranteed that we will need what others have to contribute. God has assured that His body will be a community of interdependence—we need each other. But notice what Peter says we are to do with our giftedness: "*employ it in serving one another as good stewards of the manifold grace of God.*" For God's intent to be realized, our gift must be employed, or put to work. Peter clarifies that more than just a gift, it is a steward-ship—we will answer to God for what we did with what He gave us. True fellowship is not self-serving, it focuses on meeting the needs of others. When I choose to meet someone else's needs instead of striving to meet my own, it is an act of faith. I am trusting God, and not self-effort, to meet the needs of my heart. I love the one I serve. Either I love self and serve self, or I love the Father and serve Him and those who are His. God wants His body to be a community where we all "*serve one another*" through love. An important way we serve each other is through our gifts.

📖 Looking at 1 Peter 4:11, identify the categories of ministering our gifts to each other and how God desires that to be expressed.

_____

_____

_____

_____

_____

_____

In 1 Peter 4:11, the emphasis is on the two overall categories of giftedness: speaking and serving. In a practical sense, all of us minister by speaking (what we say) and serving (what we do). God wants both of these to be done in the right manner. Whenever we speak, we should speak "*the utterances of God*"—we should say what God would say in that situation. Whenever we serve, we should do so "*by the strength that God supplies*"—we should do it in His strength, not in our own. When we say what God wants said and we serve in God's strength, the resulting fruit brings glory to God, not to us. This is God's perfect plan. We were created to glorify our Maker, not ourselves. He is the one "*to whom belongs the glory and dominion forever and ever.*"

> "*Whoever speaks, is to do so as one who is speaking the utterances of God; whoever serves is to do so as one who is serving by the strength which God supplies; so that in all things God may be glorified through Jesus Christ, to whom belongs the glory and dominion forever and ever. Amen.*" (1 Peter 4:11)

📖 Examine Ephesians 4:8 and Galatians 5:13 and record what they add to our understanding of ministering our giftedness to one another.

_____

_____

_____

_____

_____

In Ephesians 4:8 Paul quotes the Old Testament prophecy, *"When He ascended on high, He led captive a host of captives, and He gave gifts to men"* (Psalm 68:18) and interprets it as having been fulfilled by Christ giving us spiritual gifts. When Christ ascended, having saved us and forgiven our sins, He freed us from bondage to sin. He did not free us to selfishly live however we wanted, though. Galatians 5:13 teaches, *"For you were called to freedom, brethren; only do not turn your freedom into an opportunity for the flesh, but through love serve one another."*

By gifting us, God has enabled every one of us to be a minister instead of just a ministry. He gives us our talents and abilities. By His Spirit He empowers us to serve. But we must join Him. It is on us to employ our gifts in serving one another. We are called to be good stewards of his multi-faceted grace.

DAY TWO

MINISTER TO ONE ANOTHER THROUGH TOLERANCE

In one of John Wesley's sermons, the founder of the Methodist Church honestly relates a story of his own struggles with judging. Year after year he contemptuously regarded a man among his acquaintances as selfish and covetous. Aware that man possessed a good-paying job, Wesley was critical of his lack of generosity. On a particular occasion, this man contributed to one of Wesley's charities a gift that seemed very small. To the recipient it appeared quite below the man's ability to give. John Wesley's indignation knew no bounds. He raked his acquaintance back and forth with a harsh, blistering condemnation. In his diary, Wesley humbly records the man's gracious and quiet response: "I know a man who at each week's beginning goes to market and buys a penny's worth of parsnips and takes them home to boil in water, and all that week he has parsnips for his food and water for his drink; and food and drink alike cost him a penny a week." Turns out this man had been skimping in order to pay off debts he had incurred before he came to know Christ.

> *I recognize it is my own tendency to evaluate others based on what they do, while judging myself by what I intended or hoped to do. It is easy to come out on top with rules like that.*

Have you ever been guilty of becoming a spiritual fruit inspector? Are you tempted to examine the lives of others with a yardstick you don't even measure up to yourself? It is often easier to see the sins of others than it is to observe our own. I recognize it is my own tendency to evaluate others based on what they do, while judging myself by what I *intended* or hoped to do. It is easy to come out on top with rules like that. James challenges this tendency saying, *"There is only one Lawgiver and Judge, the One who is able to save and to destroy; but who are you who judge your neighbor?"* (James 4:12).

Sin separates. It fractures human relationships. It gets in the way of loving my neighbor as myself. I may not be as conscious of some of my relationship sins because they are sins of omission instead of commission. Perhaps I have neglected relationships through selfishness or avoided them because of pride and unforgiveness. I may have sinned by what I didn't do instead of by what I did. Sin happens in our relationships when Christ is not in control. As fallen people who live among other fallen people, one of the ways we can minister to one another is by making it okay to be less than perfect, and to still be in the growth process. If we want others to tolerate the imperfections in us—I know I hope for that—then it would be hypocritical to be unwilling to show forbearance and tolerance to one another.

📖 Reflect on Ephesians 4:1–3 and respond to the questions that follow.

Considering the context, what do you see as the main arena and focus of walking *"in a manner worthy"*?

_____

_____

_____

_____

What do you think it means practically to *"show tolerance to one another in love"*?

_____

_____

_____

Where does the admonition to preserve the *"unity of the Spirit"* fit in with these values?

In Ephesians 4:1–3 Paul reminds us of our responsibility to live consistently with what we profess to believe. At first glance, we may think that the call to *"walk in a manner worthy"* speaks of service, but these really are relationship verses. To *"walk worthy"* requires us to have humility and patience. It demands we *"show tolerance to one another in love."* The Greek word translated *"tolerance"* in this passage means *"to have patience with regard to the errors or weaknesses of anyone."* We learn here that we must preserve the *"unity of the Spirit."* Notice, we are not told to *produce* unity, but rather, to *preserve* it. Unity is natural when God's Spirit reigns in our hearts. We are encouraged to apply "diligence" to see that God's unity remains intact in His body. One of the unity interrupters is when we are offended by the errors or weaknesses of others and refuse to overlook them. Are you forbearing the faults of others?

📖 Look over each of the verses listed below and write your observations on what they have to say for why we need to show tolerance and what makes that hard.

Psalm 14:3

> *One of the unity interrupters is when we are offended by the errors or weaknesses of others and refuse to overlook them. Are you forbearing the faults of others?*

James 3:2

Proverbs 24:16

Why is it that we sometimes find it hard to show tolerance to one another? Obviously, there isn't one universal answer, nor is it adequate to answer simplistically by the general problem of sin. Ironically, one barrier to tolerance is our own sense of justice. Let me explain. We expect people to do the right thing. Yet Scripture makes it clear that none of us always does the right thing. Psalm 14:3 says, "... *there is no one who does good, not even one."* In James 3:2 we are reminded, "... *we all stumble in many ways."* Solomon observed, "*For a righteous man falls seven times, and rises again ..."* (Proverbs 24:16). We tend to focus on the fact that he rises, while forgetting that he also falls. Even righteous people stumble, and therefore we are in need of tolerance while we rise again. We want others to give us grace when we stumble, but is that what we do when we see others stumble? When the failure of others affects us, do we consciously acknowledge that we are all human, or do we demand a perfection from others that we know we cannot attain? It requires "*all humility* [acknowledging our own imperfections] *and gentleness, with patience"* to be "*showing tolerance for one another in love."* Think about that last phrase, "*in love."* If we do not show tolerance—have patience with the errors or weaknesses of others—we are loving conditionally with performance-based love. God wants His church to be a community where everyone has the humility, patience, and love to show tolerance for the errors and weaknesses of each other. Do you want God to only love you when you perform rightly?

📖 Take some time to meditate on Galatians 6:1-4.

What do you learn from verse 1 about helping each other bear the burden of sin?

_____

_____

_____

> *If we do not show tolerance—have patience with the errors*
> *or weaknesses of others—we are loving conditionally with*
> *performance-based love.*

According to verse 2, we "*fulfill the law of Christ"* as we bear one another's burdens. In what way?

_____

_____

_____

_____

How do you think the admonitions in verses 3–5 tie in with this context?

_____

_____

_____

We are supposed to love one another in the community of Christ, and one of the ways we love is by bearing one another's burdens. Galatians 6 begins by saying, *". . . If anyone is caught in any trespass, you who are spiritual restore such a one in a spirit of gentleness . . ."* (Galatians 6:1). We are to help each other bear the burden of sin. Genuine Christian fellowship requires that we do not ignore sin, for as Matthew 18 points out, a sinning brother or sister must repent. But we should be quick to restore, however, when repentance is evident. We all stand before God only by grace. We who are so needy of grace must be quick to give it as well. This seems to be Paul's point in the last part of verse 1: *"each one looking to yourself so that you too will not be tempted."* The focus of this exhortation is not merely that we might sin in the same way, for this would be rare. The more common danger is that in recognizing another's sin, we might respond in a sinful manner that is prideful, unforgiving, or lacking love. Paul seems to be continuing this point in verse 3: *"If anyone thinks he is something when he is nothing, he deceives himself."* We are all sinners before a holy God. Just because I might not sin in the same area as my brother or sister, or sin to the same degree, my sin put Jesus on the cross just as much as his or hers. Seeing another's stumbling affords no room for pride, for I am also "nothing" when it comes to holiness. James instructs us, *"For whoever keeps the whole law and yet stumbles in one point, he has become guilty of all"* (James 2:10). One sin is enough to make me a sinner who needs a Savior. That reality should prevent my thinking that I am superior to my brother or sister in need.

> When we "bear one another's burdens" we "fulfill the law of Christ."

When we *"Bear one another's burdens,"* we *"fulfill the law of Christ."* The early church referred to Christ's words, *"You shall love your neighbor as yourself,"* as the "royal law" (James 2:8) or the "law of Christ." The word Paul uses for "burden" isn't just talking about any difficulty, but it implies that which is beyond the normal load. While this obviously includes any burden of sin, it also includes material needs (e.g. financial burdens) as well as emotional burdens (excessive grief). Again, we see that the Christian community is to have an "others" focus. Because we are one body, when one part is hurting the whole body is affected. When I see a brother or sister carrying an extra-heavy load, I must help. The first part of Galatians 6:4 adds: *"But each one must examine his own work."* It doesn't matter what others do; I only answer to God for doing my part. Someone else's failure to love does not remove my own responsibility. Verse 5 provides an important balance to this whole idea of bearing burdens. Paul states, *"For each one will bear his own load."* I must make certain that I do not become a burden to others by not doing what I can and should. The Greek word for *"load"* here in verse 5 is different than the one translated *"burden"* in verse 2. Here, "load" refers to "my normally allotted portion or responsibility." Each of us is to carry his or her load, but we are all to help carry the *"burden"* which goes beyond normal. Are you willing to minister to one another when the load becomes too great?

MINISTER TO ONE ANOTHER BY BEING HOSPITABLE

When you think about churches today, probably your mind jumps to images of steeples and pews. The make-up of the first century church had no such trappings. There were no gargoyles over their gatherings. Even though the Temple court was woven into worship life even for the early Christians, Acts 2:46 makes it clear that kitchens and dinner tables featured prominently as well. Homes were the main place believers met. Even though most of the first believers were ethnically Jewish, they came from cultures all over the known world and from every class of society. Is it possible for people who are so very different to relate with each other and get along? The same diversity exists in the modern church. The universal body of Christ includes all shades of skin and society; all versions of politics and preference.

> *Even though the Temple court was woven into worship life even for the early Christians, Acts 2:46 makes it clear that kitchens and dinner tables featured prominently as well.*

One of the greatest (and sometimes most overlooked) tools of ministry in the modern church is also one of the simplest—the home. Maybe we can't all preach a sermon or plant a church, but we can all be hospitable. All it takes is the bare essentials. Couches or chairs and crackers and cheese create a comfortable and inviting environment to have meaningful conversations and impactful relationships. In fact, some conversations that never would happen in a church auditorium with everyone facing the front, can easily be facilitated while circled up in someone's den. Hospitality leads to community.

📖 Reflect on Peter's "one anothers" in 1 Peter 4:8–9 and write your observations on how the two times that phrase is used here connect to each other.

_____

_____

_____

_____

Be sure you don't miss how Peter starts here. He begins with, *"Above all."* The values he puts forward here are fundamental and significant. Peter admonishes us to *"keep fervent in your love for one another,"* and immediately follows this admonition with another: *"Be hospitable to one another."* One naturally flows to the other. It is hard to be *"fervent"* in your love for someone without spending time with them. Relationships require time, and so, *agapē* love of the brethren flourishes when we exercise hospitality.

The author of Hebrews admonishes, *"Let love of the brethren continue. Do not neglect to show hospitality to strangers, for by this some have entertained angels without knowing it"* (Hebrews 13:2). Peter entreats the believers to show hospitality with a good attitude;

without grumbling or complaining. Because they are opening up their homes and giving to the needs of others, there could be the temptation to murmur or complain about the ways some act. Perhaps sometimes a "stranger" might expect more than one thinks is appropriate or they may seem to take advantage of the situation or the hospitality. Peter tells us to watch out for a begrudging attitude.

📖 Examine the usage of the word "hospitality" in 1 Timothy 3:2 and Titus 1:8 and reflect on the role this plays in the function of leadership.

What comes to mind when you hear the word "hospitality"? Some men may think of it as "women's work," but that is not a biblical perspective. In fact, hospitality is one of the scriptural requirements for church leadership. In these two main passages on the qualifications of an elder, the same Greek word for "*hospitable*" we find in 1 Peter 4:8 (*philoxenos*) is used. It literally means "friend (*philos*) to strangers (*xenos*)." It refers to showing kindness and hospitality to someone who is a guest in one's house or family. In Peter and Paul's day there isn't a Holiday Inn Express® in every town or a Motel 6® leaving the light on for you. Instead, it is a priority in Jewish culture for all to have the hospitality to open up their homes to travelers.

📖 Study the verses below and identify principles from them that would be applicable to showing hospitality.

2 Corinthians 8:8 –

Here Paul reminds us that actions are a way we prove
"the sincerity of [our] love."

2 Corinthians 9:7

Speaking of giving in 2 Corinthians 8:8, Paul reminds us that actions are a way we prove *"the sincerity of [our] love."* In 2 Corinthians 9:7 he instructs that our giving should be planned and intentional. He says, *"Each one must do just as he as purposed in his heart,"* but Paul doesn't stop there. It's also about our attitude. Paul finishes saying, *"not grudgingly or under compulsion, for God loves a cheerful giver."* There really are three steps here. First, we must "purpose in our heart." We must decide to be givers, whether by time or talents or treasure. The truly hospitable person is so because of character and choice, not circumstances. But there is a second aspect to Paul's ambition for us. Good intentions aren't enough. We must follow through and "do" what we purpose. But *even that* is not enough. God wants us to purpose (be intentional), to do (take action), *and* to do what we have purposed with a good attitude. Paul uses the adjective *"cheerful"* to describe what kind of giver we are to be. The Greek word (*hilaros*) is the source of our English term "hilarious," but don't let that mislead you. The Greek term doesn't carry the idea of frivolity and being overcome with laughter associated with our English word. *Hilaros* denotes a happy, joyous, or cheerful state of mind.

📖 What does Paul's teaching in Romans 12:10 and 12:13 add to our understanding of showing hospitality to one another?

When we talk about showing hospitality, we are not simply talking about "entertaining." That can be expensive and is sometimes done just to impress others. Entertaining isn't necessarily from the heart. When we have an open heart to others, then we are willing to help where we can, which includes opening our home. It is more work, but it is worth it. We see that we are investing in relationships that matter. We are building into the lives of others, whether for a youth group or college kids, a care group or several couples. What matters is using the opportunity to show love to others. That is the heart of Romans 12:10 and 13: *"Be devoted to one another in brotherly love; give preference to one another in honor; . . . contributing to the needs of the saints, practicing hospitality."*

> *"But whoever has the world's goods, and beholds his brother in need and closes his heart against him, how does the love of God abide in him? Little children, let us not love with word or with tongue, but in deed and truth"* (1 John 3:17–18).

Let's close with the apostle John adding a final thought. *"But whoever has the world's goods, and beholds his brother in need and closes his heart against him, how does the love of God abide in him? Little children, let us not love with word or with tongue, but in deed and truth"* (1 John 3:17–18).

DAY FOUR

MINISTER TO ONE ANOTHER WITH WHAT WE SAY

Not all scriptural "One Anothers" are positive admonitions. Some tell us how <u>not</u> to treat each other. James chapter 3 makes it clear that the tongue is a powerful tool both for good and for evil. With our mouths, we can bless God and yet turn right around and with the same instrument curse people who God created in His image. No wonder James compares the tongue to a "fire." Fire can warm but also can burn. James continues the thought with example after example of creation functioning just as God designed. A fountain doesn't produce fresh and bitter water at the same time. A fig tree bears no other fruit than figs. Saltwater is only salty. Human mouths, on the other hand, don't always function as God intends. We can engage our wills to defy His design. The potential for good and evil coexists in the same orifice. They both can and do show up there. The consistency of creation condemns our inconsistency.

📖 Read James 4:11 and identify the negative "one another" and write your observations on how God views using our mouths this way in the body of Christ.

Scripture identifies believers as God's children (1 John 3:1) and the members of His church as a *"household"* (Ephesians 2:19). What does God desire in His family? James' admonishment, *"Do not speak against one another"* is a command (an imperative in the Greek), not a suggestion. The kind of *"speaking against"* referenced by James is judging our fellow brother or sister in Christ. Human pride wants to draw our own worth by comparing ourselves to those around us. When we judge, we always do so in such a way that the sin of the other is magnified and ours is belittled.

EXTRA MILE
Judging Others

When we judge others, we always do so in such a way that the sin of the other person is magnified and ours is minimized. If you have time, read Luke 18:9–14 about the Pharisee who boasts that he is not like other men. This man makes the tragic mistake of comparing himself to others rather than measuring up to God's standard. When we compare ourselves to God, none of us measure up, and humbly recognizing that is the first step to grace-filled living.

One reason God does not allow us to judge is because we are unable to do it fairly. A quotable quote attributed to Byron J. Langenfeld rings true: "Rare is the person who can weigh the faults of another without putting his finger on the scales." In 1 Corinthians 4:5 Paul shows us how God judges: He will *"bring to light the things hidden in darkness and disclose the motives of men's hearts."* We are unfit to judge because there is always something hidden we do not see, and we are unable to see the heart motive of another.

> *Rare is the person who can weigh the faults of another without putting his finger on the scales.*

📖 What clarity does James 4:12 add to this warning against judging?

_____

_____

James makes clear, *"There is only one Lawgiver and Judge."* His point here is that only the one who gave the Law has a right to hold people accountable to it. The good news here is that the Lawgiver is not only able to punish, but also to save or rescue from punishment. When we judge, we can destroy but we can never save. *"Who are you who judge your neighbor?"* Paul asks a similar question in Romans 14:4, *"Who are you to judge the servant of another? To his own master he stands or falls; and stand he will, for the Lord is able to make him stand."* We can be used of the Lord in that process, but not if our tongues are busy tearing down. Paul concludes in Romans 14:19, *"So then let us pursue the things which make for peace and the building up of one another."* We are to chase after peacemaking and building up one another. Our mouths are made for ministry, not maligning.

📖 Look at 1 Peter 3:8–9 and make note of how we are to use our mouths rightly and not wrongly.

_____

_____

_____

_____

There are many practical words of advice in this package. We are to seek harmony, have humility, avoid retaliating, and to give a blessing instead. However, it is important to realize that if the wrong things are coming off our tongues toward one another, the solution is not to "bite our tongues" and stop saying those things. James 3:8 teaches us that *"no one can tame the tongue."* The reason for this is bound in what Jesus says in Matthew 12:34: *". . . the mouth speaks out of that which fills the heart."* To change our speech, we must give our hearts over to the Lord's control. If we do, He will bless others through us.

Considering the role of what we say in this arena of ministering to one another, Scripture doesn't tell us that we can never say anything negative. While it is certainly a true statement that our tongues are meant for ministry, not maligning, this doesn't mean we only tell people words they like to hear. We are not to puff each other up with insincere flattery, nor are we to withhold truth that is needed just because it isn't wanted. In order for our tongues to produce ministry, they must speak the truth. Teaching about the body of Christ in Ephesians 4:15, Paul identifies that we are to be *"speaking the truth in love"* to each other. Notice, we are to *speak*, not remain silent. We are to speak truth, not flattery or opinion. And we are to do so in love. When we do this, we each *"grow up in all aspects into Him who is the Head, even Christ."* To use our mouths for ministry, we must be willing to say hard things to each other when warranted. In Romans 15:14 Paul writes, *"And concerning you, my brethren, I myself also am convinced that you yourselves are full of goodness, filled with all knowledge, and able also to admonish one another."*

> To use our mouths for ministry, we must be willing to say hard
> things to each other when warranted.

📖 How do Proverbs 27:5–6 and Ephesians 4:25 bring balance to our view of ministering with our mouths?

In Proverbs 27:5–6 Solomon advises, *"Better is open rebuke than love that is concealed. Faithful are the wounds of a friend, but deceitful are the kisses of an enemy."* Solomon is saying that to speak, even if the words are hard, is better than to conceal our love for one another with silence. Sometimes the most loving speech is open rebuke. When we do not say what needs to be said, or when we speak insincere words to another out of fear or cowardice, we are being an enemy, rather than their friend. Jesus says, *"Greater love has no one than this, that one lay down his life for his friends"* (John 15:13). We need to be willing to lay ourselves down and speak up. Paul continues in Ephesians 4:25, *". . . laying aside falsehood, speak truth, each one of you, with his neighbor, for we are members of one another."*

Day Five

For Me to Follow God

If I have food stuck between my teeth or my clothing is somehow out of sorts, I want someone to point it out. They are not being a friend to me if they see a problem and say nothing. Paul says he is convinced we are *"able to admonish one another."* The word "admonish" means to warn or to exhort. The Greek word literally means "to place before the mind." When we admonish one another, we are not responsible for what the other does with what we say. We can only put it before their minds and leave the response to them and to the work of God's Spirit. But if we remain silent, we may be working against their growth instead of for it. There is an important point to catch in Paul's words here. He is convinced the Romans are able to admonish each other because he is convinced they are *"full of goodness"* and *"filled with all knowledge."* These are two important prerequisites to admonishing one another. First, we must be full of goodness. Before we speak, we must make sure our heart is right. Jesus instructed, *"first take the log out of your own eye, and then you will see clearly to take the speck out of your brother's eye"* (Matthew 7:5). Second, to admonish rightly we must be filled with *all* knowledge. This isn't saying we have to know everything about everything. It is saying we need to know the whole story before we speak. Proverbs 12:18 says, *"There is one who speaks rashly like the thrusts of a sword."* When we speak without thinking we can do a lot of damage. Proverbs 20:25 says, *"It is a trap for a man to say rashly, 'It is holy!', and after the vows to make inquiry."* Proverbs 18:17 says, *"The first to plead his case seems right, until another comes and examines him."* Make sure you have heard both sides of the story before you try and admonish your brother.

> *"Before we speak, we must make sure our heart is right. Jesus instructed, "first take the log out of your own eye, and then you will see clearly to take the speck out of your brother's eye."*
> *(Matthew 7:5)*

Over the course of this week's study, we have considered many different "one another" passages under this theme umbrella of ministering to one another. God wants His body to be a community where through love, we all *"serve one another."* We have looked at using our unique giftedness to minister. We have considered the role of tolerating each other's imperfections and incompleteness. We have reflected on the important role hospitality plays in ministry to each other. And we have looked at key passages on loving enough to admonish and speak the hard things.

What are some evidences of His working through you for the benefit of others?

_____

_____

_____

_____

What do you think your main spiritual gifts might be?

_____

_____

_____

How can you develop your giftedness?

_____

_____

_____

_____

Honestly reflect on the list below and check the areas you think are strengths for you and circle the ones you know you need to work on.

___ Minister to one another with our gifts

___ Ministering to one another through tolerance

___ Ministering to one another through hospitality

___ Ministering to one another with what we say

In John 15:7–8 Jesus says, *"If you abide in Me, and My words abide in you, ask whatever you wish, and it will be done for you. My Father is glorified by this, that you bear much fruit, and so prove to be My disciples."* It is a classic cause-effect statement that speaks directly to this goal of ministering to one another. If you think of these verses as a pyramid, bearing *"much fruit"* rests on the foundation of an abiding relationship with Christ and emersion in His truth. Even the terminology is important. We don't minister to one another to be better Christians or earn favor with God. Our ministry and service are to be the fruit of our walk with God. Like all fruit, the more the plant matures, the more fruit it will bear. Do not be discouraged if you long for more fruit than is yet evident.

We don't minister to one another to be better Christians or earn favor with God. Our ministry and service are to be the fruit of our walk with God.

📖 Consider the five areas of John 15:7–8 and rate how you think you are doing.

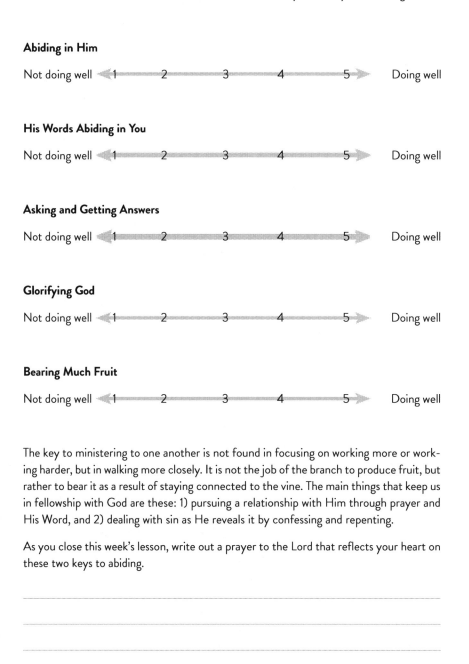

Abiding in Him

Not doing well — 1 — 2 — 3 — 4 — 5 — Doing well

His Words Abiding in You

Not doing well — 1 — 2 — 3 — 4 — 5 — Doing well

Asking and Getting Answers

Not doing well — 1 — 2 — 3 — 4 — 5 — Doing well

Glorifying God

Not doing well — 1 — 2 — 3 — 4 — 5 — Doing well

Bearing Much Fruit

Not doing well — 1 — 2 — 3 — 4 — 5 — Doing well

The key to ministering to one another is not found in focusing on working more or working harder, but in walking more closely. It is not the job of the branch to produce fruit, but rather to bear it as a result of staying connected to the vine. The main things that keep us in fellowship with God are these: 1) pursuing a relationship with Him through prayer and His Word, and 2) dealing with sin as He reveals it by confessing and repenting.

As you close this week's lesson, write out a prayer to the Lord that reflects your heart on these two keys to abiding.

....

....

....

_____

_____

_____

_____

_____

_____

_____

_____

_____

_____

_____

Works Cited

1. William Manchester, *Last Lion: Winston Spencer Churchill: Visions of Glory 1847–1932* (Boston: Little, Brown, and Company, 1983.

NOTES

LESSON 4

PRAYING FOR ONE ANOTHER

James is the apostle who was nicknamed "camel knees" because of the callouses formed from years of devotion to prayer. He is the one who stated, *"The effective prayer of a righteous man can accomplish much"* (James 5:16). He begins the verse, though, by saying, *"Therefore, confess your sins to one another, and pray for one another, so that you may be healed."* When he calls us to *"pray for one another,"* it is an imperative statement in the original language; a command, if you will. It is not a suggestion. Also, the Greek verb there is in the present tense. That means we are to continually pray for each other, not just pray once and forget it. God wants His church to be a community that is connected to each other and dependent on Him. The word James uses that is translated *"pray"* here is *euchomai* and has the idea of a strong desire for someone—to express a wish. Consider the relational implications of this. We should be involved in each other's lives so that we know how to pray for each other. We should care enough to be able to recognize the needs of those in our lives and to have developed a "wish" for their good. If so, we will be motivated to express that wish to the One who can do something about it. Communicating that awareness to God is to be an habitual manifestation of our dependence on Him. We recognize what we are unable to do, and we exercise faith in what He is able to do. You see, praying for each other is a three-way exchange: God, the other person, and me. The other person has a need. If it is worthy of prayer, it is beyond that person's ability to address. I also have a need. God desires that we live in moment-by-moment dependence on Him. Therefore, I must pray so that I entrust every need to God instead of leaving it to the other person or entrusting it to myself. If the church is to be a body, then there are times when I am supposed to hurt. I need to mourn with those who are mourning. When the church is a "one another" community, we all share in the pleasures of each *and* the pains of each as well. James even instructs *"confess your sins to one another."* We need to be open enough with each other—even to the point of sharing our faults—so that our truest and deepest needs are known. We must be willing to be vulnerable with one another.

Therefore, confess your sins to one another, and pray for one another,
so that you may be healed. The effective prayer of a righteous man
can accomplish much." (James 5:16)

I have learned that prayer is one of the ways God knits the body together. When I am praying for another, I develop compassion for their predicament. To pray rightly, I must place myself in their shoes. While this influences how I pray, it also affects how I view and relate with them. God knows that. He desires that our lives be connected to Him *and* to each other. In the above passage, James promises that "*the effective prayer of a righteous man can accomplish much.*" The Greek word for prayer here (*deesis*) is entirely different than the one first mentioned. This word carries the idea of acknowledging a need and asking God to meet that need. What a beautiful consideration when we think of one another! We should have a strong desire for God to work in the lives of those around us. We should want to see His will accomplished, and His joy and peace made real in their lives. As we see needs that the person cannot meet—needs that only God can truly meet in the right way and at the right time—we call to the Lord on their behalf. If we can learn to pray with this kind of care for one another, we will often see heaven on earth. That is what God wants. He wants His will in each life. He wants each of us admitting that we cannot meet the needs we see. He wants us coming to Him to meet the needs His way since He knows best in *every situation* for *each person.* How aware are you of the needs around you in the body? How open are you with your own needs?

DAY ONE

WHY SHOULD WE PRAY FOR ONE ANOTHER?

Have you ever stopped to reflect on the reality of difficulties in our lives? We live in a fallen world, and so it is not surprising that needs exist. The sins and selfishness of people guarantees that everything will not go as God designed or originally intended. Yet we are not left alone; we are loved and watched over by the omnipotent, all-powerful God. He is able to release every burden, repair every wound, meet every need, and remove every obstacle. Not only is God omnipotent, He is omniscient—all-knowing. Nothing that comes our way ever catches Him by surprise. No need of ours ever escapes His notice. No wistful longing or desperate heart cry is foreign to Him. To that truth must be added the certainty that God is omnipresent—able to be everywhere. He is never too far away to catch us or too distracted to notice us or too busy to get around to us. To these incredible attributes must be added the fact that He loves us completely and unconditionally. So, if all of this is true, why do we even need to pray? Why are our needs not met even before they become needs? Certainly, God is able to intervene.

God has designed our world in such a way that we can
actually make a difference, not only by our own actions, but also
by our asking.

We usually reconcile such spiritual dilemmas with reminders that God is sovereign and we must trust that He knows best. And yet, taken too far, this line of thinking actually undermines praying for each other at all. If "God is going to do what He is going to do regardless of what we pray," then why should we bother praying at all? The answer is simple—we are commanded to pray. That truth carries with it several fundamental realities. One, our biblical calls to pray make it clear that God wants us to pray. Two, they also make it clear that our praying matters. It makes a difference. Often, we are guilty of ignoring our part in the equation. God has designed our world in such a way that we can actually make a difference, not only by our own actions, but also by our asking. The apostle James states it simply: ". . . *you do not have because you do not ask*" (James 4:2). While the ability to pray does not endow us with limitless power—God can say "no" if He deems it appropriate—prayer can and does change things. And clearly, there are times when God refuses to act without involving us.

📖 Read 2 Corinthians 1:8 and write out all the ways the Apostle Paul describes the afflictions he and his companions experienced in Asia.

In this passage we see that God does allow even His greatest servants to be hard pressed with difficulty. The term Paul uses for affliction—*thlipsis*—means to press, to squeeze, to crush. Listen to how Paul describes their experience in Asia. He and his traveling companions were "*burdened excessively.*" They were taken beyond their strength. It got so bad at some point during their difficulties that Paul says they "*despaired even of life.*" Either death looked better than what they were going through, or they had lost hope for any other outcome.

📖 Examine 2 Corinthians 1:9 and identify why Paul believed God allowed them to go through their difficulties.

Paul would be less than human if he were unbothered by their difficulties, but he also had come to a place of recognizing that the adversity brought a good result as well. It made them unable to trust in themselves to deliver. The situation was beyond their control. That may not sound good, but it made them put their trust in God instead of themselves. As Geoffrey Bull says, "self-reliance, is God-defiance." He doesn't want us to be able to handle life by ourselves.

"Self-reliance, is God-defiance."

—Geoffrey Bull

📖 Take a look at 2 Corinthians 1:10. What had Paul experienced in the past that gave him confidence in the present and future?

_____

_____

_____

_____

Whether in the immediate or distant past, Paul references that he and his companions had faced death before and been delivered. Often in Acts we read accounts of God protecting and rescuing Paul and others from life-threatening circumstances. When Paul speaks of God as *"He on whom we have set our hope,"* he is still waiting for deliverance from his present distress. *"And He will yet deliver us,"* was his expectation.

📖 Read 2 Corinthians 1:11 and identify how Paul could be so confident that God would deliver?

_____

_____

_____

_____

How could he be so confident? Because he had people praying for him. Paul began these verses by stating he didn't want the Corinthians *"to be unaware, brethren, of our affliction."* He wanted them to be aware because he needed them to pray for him. I wonder how many times our deliverance has been delayed because we were not willing to share the need with the body. We didn't let our need be known or request the needed prayers. God can do whatever He wants whenever He wants, but sometimes He chooses to wait for us to exercise the faith of casting our cares on Him before He intervenes. God wants His church to be a community where we bear each other's burdens in prayer because *"we, who are many, are one body in Christ, and individually members one of another"* (Romans 12:5).

Did you notice what Paul reveals here about the impact of the Corinthian prayers? Their intercession was more than just moral support. He says to them, *"you also joining in helping us through your prayers."* When we pray for one another, do we believe that our prayers make a difference? We should, because they do. One of the reasons God wants to work through our joining with others in supplication is so that we all get to rejoice in the answers. Paul's expectation is *"that thanks may be given by many persons on our behalf for the favor bestowed upon us through the prayers of many."* Did you catch that last phrase? He said there was *"favor bestowed upon us through the prayers of the many."* But what if "the many" *weren't* praying? God wants us to "own" the hardships of others in the body. He wants us to pray for one another so He can bestow favor through our prayers. Paul did think it was important to acknowledge that God was the one who would *"yet deliver,"* but the Corinthians had the privilege of joining God in what He wanted to do in the lives of others. We have that privilege as well. God wants us joining Him through prayer. Is there someone you can bestow favor on through prayer? God may be waiting for you to join Him before their deliverance is sent.

> *". . . that thanks may be given by many persons on our behalf for the favor bestowed upon us through the prayers of many"*
> (2 Corinthians 1:11)

DAY TWO

HOW SHOULD WE PRAY FOR ONE ANOTHER?

Years ago, the English missionary doctor, Helen Roseveare, shared an example of answered prayer from her experience as a missionary in central Africa:

> A mother at our mission station died after giving birth to a premature baby. We tried to improvise an incubator to keep the infant alive, but the only hot water bottle we had was beyond repair. So we asked the children to pray for the baby and for her sister. One of the girls responded. "Dear God, please send a hot water bottle today. Tomorrow will be too late because by then the baby will be dead. And dear Lord, send a doll for the sister so she won't feel so lonely." That afternoon a large package arrived from England. The children watched eagerly as we opened it. Much to their surprise, under some clothing was a hot water bottle! Immediately the girl who had prayed so earnestly started to dig deeper, exclaiming, "If God sent that, I'm sure He also sent a doll!" And she was right! The heavenly Father knew in advance of that child's sincere requests, and 5 months earlier He had led a ladies' group to include both of those specific articles.

God, who hears our prayers, is not limited by time and distance. Because of this, our prayers are not hindered or inhibited by either of these. Through the gift of supplication, we can enter into the needs of others. We can travel great distances on our knees. Having been endowed with such power, we are in danger of living as practical atheists when we faithlessly pray in such generic terms as, "Oh Lord, bless them," without asking for anything specific. We stand in the suburbs of blasphemy when we ask God for so little and trust him for such insignificant and immeasurable details in our prayers for others.

📖 Read Ephesians 6:18. The word "all" is used four times in Ephesians 6:18, and each use instructs us about prayer. Consider each of these phrases in the larger context and write down your thoughts on how this applies to the believer.

"With all prayer and petition..."

The Four "Alls" of Prayer

"With all prayer and petition pray at all times in the Spirit, and with this in view, be on the alert with all perseverance and petition for all the saints." (Ephesians 6:18)

The first "all" of prayer—"*all prayer and petition*"—is given in the context of taking up the "*sword of the Spirit,*" which is the Word of God. In light of this, all our praying and petitioning must be "*in the Spirit.*" Prayer is talking with God. This may sound overly simplistic, but it is easily forgotten. Prayer is a conversation between our spirit and the Spirit of God. But if I am not careful, it can become a habit or ritual of speaking words that do not make it past the ceiling. What constitutes true prayer is not determined by folded hands, closed eyes, or bowed heads. True prayer happens when I am honestly praying from my heart and I am really talking to God. Sometimes what we call prayer is merely talking to ourselves in religious jargon or talking to the others around us in spiritual sounding sermonettes. Real prayer is talking with God and God alone.

"*. . . pray at all times in the Spirit.*" Look at this phrase from Ephesians 6:18 and consider how Hebrews 13:5 and 1 Thessalonians 5:17 add to this thought.

The second "all" of prayer is that I am to "*pray at all times.*" Prayer is not reserved for a special hour of the day or a special meeting on the church calendar. God intends our praying to be an ongoing, unending conversation between us and the one who will never leave us (Hebrews 13:5). The apostle Paul urged the Thessalonian believers, "*pray without ceasing*" (1 Thessalonians 5:17). That is not possible if prayer is something which occurs at a particular hour or a meeting. But it is possible if it is something which happens in our hearts. We can converse with Christ as we walk, as we wait, as we work, and even as we worry—especially then. From the time we awaken, we should be talking with the Lord. This kind of praying isn't meant for flowery words or long monologues. It may be as simple as saying, "Lord, I need your help." When are we to pray? At all times.

". . . *and with this in view, be on the alert with all perseverance.* Record your thoughts on this phrase.

The third "all" of prayer is *"with all perseverance."* Prayer is not preparation for the work of ministry; it is the work of ministry, and believe me, it is work. The great preacher and intercessor R. A. Torrey wrote,

> *Why is it that God does not give to us the things that we ask,*
> *the first time we ask? The answer is plain: He would do us the*
> *far greater good of training us in persistent faith...Oh, men and*
> *women, pray through; pray through; pray through! Do not just*
> *begin to pray and pray a little while and throw up your hands and*
> *quit; but pray and pray and pray until God bends the heavens and*
> *comes down!"*

". . . *and petition for all the saints.*" Compare this phrase with 1 Corinthians 12:25 and Matthew 5:44.

The fourth "all" of prayer is *"petition for all the saints."* Prayer is not to be selfish or self-serving. God wants His body to be a community that cares for one another through prayers for one another. If the only needs I discuss are my own, I am not praying the way God wants. He wants us to be lifting up each other. This even includes the ones I don't like—especially those. If my attitude toward a fellow brother or sister is stained or strained, praying for them helps both of us immensely. In 1 Corinthians 12:25, Paul puts forward the goal that *"there may be no division in the body, but that the members may have the same care for one another."* We need to pray for those we don't want to pray for. In the Sermon on the Mount, Jesus said, *"But I say to you, love your enemies and pray for those who persecute you"* (Matthew 5:44). Through prayer, we can work to turn enemies into friends.

DAY THREE

WHAT GETS IN THE WAY OF PRAYING FOR ONE ANOTHER?

The early church had little clout with the culture of their day. When society treated them with disrespect or disdain, they could organize no boycott or protest. When persecution arose, they had no army to defend themselves from harm. When the governing officials sanctioned that persecution, the followers of Christ had no legislators or lobbyists to plead on their behalf. That does not indicate, however, that they were powerless. Through prayer, they could lay their concerns before Almighty God, and pray they did. As persecution heated up, so did their prayer meetings. At one point, Herod the king arrested the apostle Peter with the intention of putting him to death. The church couldn't *pull* him out of jail, but they could *pray* him out. As Peter slept what was supposed to have been his last night on earth, *"prayer for him was being made fervently by the church to God"* (Acts 12:5). In those pre-dawn hours, the Lord sent an angel who removed Peter's chains and escorted him unseen from prison. At first Peter thought he was having a vision, but when the angel left him outside, he realized what had happened. When he came to Mary's house, he understood how—God's people were praying for him. Acts 12:12 states, *"he went to the house of Mary, the mother of John who was also called Mark, where many were gathered together and were praying."*

> *"...prayer for him was being made fervently by the church to God."*
> (Acts 12:5)

God has not changed, but have we? In this modern day, do we have so many other options that we neglect fervent prayer?

> *We will only advance in our work as fast and as far as we advance*
> *on our knees. Prayer opens the channel between a soul and God;*
> *prayerlessness increases it. That is why prayer is so exhausting*
> *and so vital. If we believed it, the prayer meeting would be as full*
> *as the church.*
>
> —Alan Redpath

But our prayer meetings aren't full. Perhaps it is because we are not aware of our brother or sister's need as we should be, or maybe it is because we don't believe God is willing and able to intervene. Jim Elliot was eventually martyred as he attempted to take the gospel to an Ecuadorian tribe. He said this about the prayers of others on his behalf: "I have felt the impact of your prayer in these past weeks. I am certain now that nothing has more powerful influence on this life of mine than your prayers." Could he have laid his life on the altar without the prayer support of others? But we do not pray as we should, in part, because we do not care about other's circumstances as we should. It may be that we need others to pray *for us* in this area of our concern for and connection with each other. Paul prayed this for the Thessalonians: "*may the Lord cause you to increase and abound in love for one another*" (1 Thessalonians 3:12).

Perhaps the reason we do not pray as we should is not from lack of concern or lack of faith in God's ability, but from a lack of confidence in our own prayers. However feeble, our prayers are powerful because God to whom we pray is powerful. We may not fully see the effect of our prayers this side of heaven, but I suspect there will be plenty of encouragement there as we look back on our prayers here. Edith Schaeffer wrote,

> . . . we all have to wait until the astonishing discoveries will one day be made, and find out whose faithful prayer in hospitals, prisons, jungles, wheelchairs, crowded city apartments, cabins in the woods, farms, factories or concentration camps has been a part of a specific victory in snatching someone from a circle of death, or in breaking chains so that there seems to be an ease for that one in stepping into new life. I feel sure that we'll be surprised beyond measure to discover who or how many will receive the rewards for their part in taking literally and with simple faith and trust the responsibility to intercede, to pray, to make requests day in and day out.

📖 What point is Samuel making in 1 Samuel 12:23 about how important it is to pray for one another?

_____

_____

_____

_____

_____

Have you ever told someone, "I'll be praying for you" and didn't? My guess is that we all have done this many times. Our intentions are good, but memory and other distractions may inhibit intentions from becoming reality. We may feel a moment of guilt when we see the person, or we may forget about the incident altogether. We probably wouldn't think of our neglect as "sin." That is what makes Samuel's words here so intriguing. He speaks of his potential failure to pray for the people of Israel as a sin, and not just a sin against Israel. He calls it a sin against God. The context of Samuel's words here are the transition from the period of the judges to the time of the kings and prophets. Samuel was really the bridge between those two eras, serving as the last judge and the first prophet as the first king was installed. Look at the words Samuel uses to convey his heart. Samuel considered it sin to ever stop praying for Israel. We often think of sin as something wrong that we do, but here Samuel defines sin as being something left undone. Are we guilty of the sin of unspoken supplication?

How does the example of 1 Thessalonians 5:25, 2 Thessalonians 3:1, and Hebrews 13:18 speak to the needs of spiritual leaders?

_____

_____

_____

_____

Praying for one another helps cement our love for each other.

There are many VIP's in our life for whom God would have us to pray. Obviously, we should pray for our family and cherished friends. No one will pray as passionately for them as we would. We see from Samuel's example that we must pray regularly for those under our spiritual charge. Perhaps the Lord has given us a Bible study group or Sunday School class, or we may be in charge of a church. Even if we aren't, we should pray for the one to which we belong. We see Paul and other spiritual leaders repeatedly say, *"Pray for us"* (e.g. 1 Thessalonians 5:25, 2 Thessalonians 3:1, Hebrews 13:18, etc.). We have a responsibility to pray for those who lead us spiritually, as well as those whom we lead. We also have a vested interest, for if they are doing well, we benefit, and if they are not, we suffer. We lose the benefit we would have if God were ministering to us through them, or we add the burden of more needed ministry and concern if they are under our charge. This kind of praying is what I call "prayer along the vertical line." We are to pray for those over us and for those under us.

📖 Reflect on 2 Thessalonians 1:3 and the need to pray for our fellow Christians.

_____

_____

_____

_____

_____

_____

The vertical line of prayer is important, but it is not the only one that should shape our praying. As we are seeing in the "One Another" commands, there is a horizontal line with which we should also be concerned. We should pray for one another—our fellow Christians. Writing to the Thessalonians, Paul talked of his prayers of thanks for them: *"We ought always to give thanks to God for you, brethren . . . because your faith is greatly enlarged, and the love of each one of you toward one another grows ever greater."* Praying for one another helps cement our love for each other.

God wants His church to be a community where we don't just say we will pray for each other; we really do pray. This is especially true if they ask us to pray. When someone asks me to pray for them, I always try to either pray with them right then if appropriate, or to start praying as soon as the conversation has ended. Our supplication matters. We may not always see the difference, but it always makes a difference. Revelation 5:8 speaks of *"golden bowls full of incense, which are the prayers of the saints."* These are kept in the presence of the Lord in heaven. That idea ought to motivate us away from the sin of unspoken supplication.

> *"Keep watching and praying that you may not come into temptation; the spirit is willing, but the flesh is weak." (Mark 14:38)*

DAY FOUR

PERSISTING IN PRAYER TOGETHER

"When they [the disciples] had entered the city, they went up to the upper room where they were staying. . . . These all with one mind were continually devoting themselves to prayer" (Acts 1:13–14). Jesus' words to the disciples before His ascension had neither been vague nor ambiguous. Wait! Ten days separated His ascension and the coming of the Holy Spirit. The disciples spent those days praying. When we pray, rest assured there will be times when we have to wait for the answer. It is frustrating how often that word "wait" appears in Scripture, but there is much spirituality woven into this simple term. When you think about it, much of life is spent waiting. But waiting is not something we do until life happens; it is part of life. We can accept that most of our prayers are not answered instantly. We struggle when God takes longer to act than we think He should. I believe God has purpose in the waiting part of prayer. There is something in waiting that draws our eyes to Him where they should be. The longer we pray, the more God reshapes what we are praying for and molds it toward His will.

One danger when we are waiting on a response to our prayers is to lose heart and stop praying. When God doesn't answer right away, we think we have wasted our time. Horatius Bonar reminds us,

> No prayer is lost. Praying breath was never spent in vain. There is no such thing as prayer unanswered or unnoticed by God, and some things that we count as refusals or denials are simply delays.

In this passage we find that the disciples were "continually devoting themselves" to prayer—a strong expression denoting persistence. Perhaps God's delay was so they would persist. Sooner or later, each one of us finds ourselves in the place of waiting. One practical lesson we glean from Acts chapter 1 is that it is easier to be devoted to prayer with others than alone. These disciples prayed together. Not only is praying together a help and encouragement to you, it is also a ministry to the other person. God wants His body to be a community that fervently prays for one another.

How does the encounter between Jesus and His disciples in Mark 14:37–38 reflect the weaknesses of human nature and our need to persist in prayer?

....

....

....

....

> *The great thrust of world missions, the first missionary journey of*
> *Paul and Barnabas, was born in a season of prayer, not a planning*
> *meeting.*

As Jesus prayed in Gethsemane, He asked the disciples to stay and pray with Him. Unfortunately, they weren't very persistent. In Mark 14:37–38 we read,

> *"And He came and found them sleeping, and said to Peter, 'Simon,*
> *are you asleep? Could you not keep watch for one hour?' Keep*
> *watching and praying that you may not come into temptation; the*
> *spirit is willing, but the flesh is weak."*

We need each other if we are to *"keep watching and praying."* Maybe there is a prayer meeting or prayer chain at your church that you could get connected with. Or perhaps you could ask another believer to join with you as a prayer partner.

📖 Review Acts 1:13–14 and write your thoughts on why Jesus thought it important for His followers to wait and pray.

....

....

....

....

The ten days between the ascension of Jesus and Pentecost represented "wait training" for the disciples. An important part of this "wait training" was focused prayer. It is this unseen activity that makes such a difference in each of our situations. E. M. Bounds states, "It is true that Bible prayers in word and print are short, but the praying men of the Bible were with God through many a sweet and holy wrestling hour. They won by few words but long waiting." Waiting on the Lord focuses us in making sure we are seeking God and staying sensitive to Him. Likely part of that time in the Upper Room was praying *for* one another—that is our theme this week—but an important point not to miss is that they were praying *with* one another. God wants His body to be a community that waits before Him in unified prayer.

📖 What do the following verses instruct us about our mindset as we pray together?

Romans 12:16

Romans 15:5

It is clear that the early church prayed together. Such praying makes a difference in us as a body. Luke records in Acts 1 that they prayed "*with one mind.*" Paul twice exhorted the Romans to "*be of the same mind toward one another*" (Romans 12:16; 15:5). One of the benefits of praying with one another is that God knits our hearts together in unity. I wonder how much opportunity to grow together the modern church misses because praying together is not a priority!

DAY FIVE

FOR ME TO FOLLOW GOD

> *We never know how God will answer our prayers, but we can*
> *expect that He will get us involved in His plan for the answer. If we*
> *are true intercessors, we must be ready to take part in God's work*
> *on behalf of the people for whom we pray.*
>
> —Corrie Ten Boom

It is worth noticing that the great thrust of world missions, the first missionary journey of Paul and Barnabas, was born in a season of prayer, not a planning meeting. Acts 13:2 records, *"While they were ministering to the Lord and fasting, the Holy Spirit said, 'Set apart for Me Barnabas and Saul for the work to which I have called them.' "* The leaders were worshiping and fasting. The Greek word translated *"ministering"* here is *leitourgeo* from which we get our English term "liturgy." It is in the present tense, indicating ongoing action. The emphasis seems to be that they were in a season of worship and seeking the Lord as the ministry continued. We don't know the catalyst for their fast, but it was during it that God chose to speak. As we pray for one another, our conversation is not supposed to be one-sided. God wants us to listen to Him, not just read to Him a list of things we want. God's message was clear and unequivocal: He wanted to reassign two of the key leaders in the church. The most obvious reason for the direction of travel Barnabas and Saul chose is the fact that they were *"sent out by the Holy Spirit."* We trust that not only was the task divinely initiated, but the process as well. We know that Barnabas was originally from Cyprus (Acts 4:36) and would have been familiar with the culture and area. Seleucia was the seaport of Antioch and was the logical route to Cyprus. Think about the implications of this. Antioch was the first primarily Gentile church. We learn in Acts 11:20 that this church was planted by Christians originally from Cyprus. Obviously, they would be burdened for their fellow Gentiles to come to know the life-changing message of the gospel. Being from Cyprus, no doubt Barnabas was burdened to pray for his native land. It is logical to assume that they were praying for God to save their countrymen. In the midst of their prayers, God calls them to take part in answering them.

One of the reasons God wants His church to be a community that prays for one another is that through prayer our hearts are drawn toward His will for the object of our prayers. As we are involved in ministering to them by praying for them, we are most open to God inviting us to minister to them in other ways. Corrie ten Boom's faith was molded in the Nazi concentration camps of World War II. She offers this advice on praying for one another:

> We never know how God will answer our prayers, but we can expect
> that He will get us involved in His plan for the answer. If we are true
> intercessors, we must be ready to take part in God's work on behalf of
> the people for whom we pray.

As we pray for one another, we must be willing to participate in the answer to those prayers. If we are praying for a need that we have the ability to meet, we need to stop praying and start acting in faith that God will use us to be the answer. If we are willing to pray, but not willing to act, have we not failed to *"love one another, just as He commanded us"* (1 John 3:23)? We are like the Christians whose faith James condemns in James 2:15-17. He admonishes,

> *"If a brother or sister is without clothing and in need of daily*
> *food, and one of you says to them, "Go in peace, be warmed and*
> *be filled," and yet you do not give them what is necessary for their*

body, what use is that? Even so faith, if it has no works, is dead,
being by itself."

True prayer is an expression of faith, but it cannot be the only way we are willing to show our faith.

Prayer is conversation with God.

- Clement of Alexandria

What are some current situations where you can learn of needs among your Christian brothers and sisters for which you can pray?

_____

_____

_____

_____

_____

Do you consider yourself a praying Christian? Why, or why not?

_____

_____

_____

_____

How could you become more prayerful?

_____

_____

_____

_____

_____

Which obstacles (practical, spiritual, emotional, etc.) keep you from praying as much as you feel you should for others (check the ones that apply)?

___ Not confident in prayer

___ Unaware of needs

___ Don't have a healthy concern for others

___ Unsure of how to word my prayers

___ Haven't studied what the Bible teaches on prayer

___ Lack of good models to follow

___ Other:

How has your view on praying for others changed as a result of this lesson?

What are some prayer needs you have and with whom can you share them?

In Philippians 4:6 Paul states, "*Be anxious for nothing, but in everything by prayer and supplication with thanksgiving let your requests be made known to God.*" In other words, "don't worry about anything; instead, pray about everything, and don't forget to thank God for the answers." Paul continues in verse 7 telling us what will result if we pray in this way: "*And the peace of God, which surpasses all comprehension, will guard your hearts and your minds in Christ Jesus.*" The early church father, Clement of Alexandria, said, "Prayer is conversation with God." Ask the Lord to bring to your mind some needs around you. Make a list and then close out this week's lesson by talking to the Lord about them.

(blank lined writing space)

Works Cited

1. Rich Buhler, "A Dying Baby, a Hot Water Bottle, a Child's Prayer, and a Children's Doll—Truth!" _Truth or Fiction_, March 17, 2015, https://ww.truthorfiction.com/hotwaterbottle/.

2. Edith Schaeffer, as quoted in "Inspiration for Missions," _Mark Perkins—the Person_ (blog), October 6, 2011, http://perkinsfirm.blogspot.com/2011/

NOTES

LESSON 5

FORGIVING ONE ANOTHER

Fracturing. We have all seen it. We have all experienced it to one degree or another. We may have been guilty participants. Fractured families, fractured friendships, fractured churches, fractured communities—all of these are the consequences not just of offenses, but of not being able to move beyond them—of not forgiving offenses. Whether in a marriage, in a family or in a church group, it is certain that at some point there will be conflict. Solomon tells us in Proverbs 27:17 that *"As iron sharpens iron, so one person sharpens another"* (NIV). While the adage reflects the benefit of relationships (sharpening) it is important to remember that "iron on iron" also produces friction and heat. I have often said that the only fellow with all his troubles behind him is a school bus driver. Conflict will come, and if it is not dealt with in a healthy way, it can be the death of true community. Divisions and schisms in churches and families can cause great pain and can last for generations. God's solution is not to blindly hope for perfect people, perfect organizations, and perfect relationships. Those are impossible expectations in a fallen world and will only be found in heaven. In the meantime, we are called to be givers of forgiveness as those who have been forgiven much by Christ. God wants His body to be a community that is characterized by showing the grace of forgiveness to one another.

I have often taken engaged couples through a preparation for marriage course—an important investment of time for the soon-to-be-married. As a pastor, I have had my share of counseling sessions with couples whose relationship is on the rocks, and I would far rather spend time working on safety precautions at the top of the cliff than run a rescue station at the bottom of it. Sessions with those headed to the altar are much more enjoyable (and much less stressful) than those for whom the altar is a distant memory and forgotten commitment. The soon-to-be married couples are always in love and almost always young and naïve. Amid all the instruction, one piece of practical advice I always offer is this: The key to maintaining the intimacy you now enjoy is the ability to ask for and to grant forgiveness quickly. Usually my sage wisdom is met with polite smiles, but I suspect behind them is the erroneous idea that such counsel is probably good for some people, but "we" won't be needing that. I consider the essential advice as an investment in the future, and I hope it comes back to mind when the realities of relationship burst their bubble of romantic notions.

God wants His body to be a community that is characterized by
showing the grace of forgiveness to one another.

DAY ONE

FELLOWSHIP WITH ONE ANOTHER

Personally, I think one of the most amazing realities of the book of Genesis is that even in the perfection of Eden before the fall there could be something that was "not good." Genesis 2:18 states, *"Then the Lord God said, 'It is not good for man to be alone; I will make him a helper suitable for him.'"* Sin had not yet left its stain, but still, all was not good. Man enjoyed perfect fellowship with God, yet he was still not complete. What a contrast with the continuous refrain of creation up to this point; seven times in chapter 1 we read *"and God saw that it was good"* (1:4, 10, 12, 18, 21, 25, 31). But it was not good for man to be alone. He was made with a God-given need for relationships. He was created incomplete so that God could complete him with Eve. She was to be *"a helper suitable for him."* But beyond that, there would be children, and eventually friends and neighbors. God made humankind as social creatures with a need for Him and for each other.

Why did God create man alone? Why didn't He create Adam and Eve at the same time? Eve certainly wasn't an afterthought. Perhaps God waited to make Eve in part because Adam needed to become aware of his need for relationships. In Genesis 2:19 God creates the beasts of the field and the birds of the sky and brings them to Adam. Yet these could not fill the need of his heart. Genesis 2:20b tells us, *"but for Adam there was not found a helper suitable for him."* This was not a case of divine trial and error. The season of single-ness had purpose in Adam's life. He needed to see what he really needed, and he needed to learn that it was from his creator that he would see his needs met. One of the most powerful phrases in this chapter is *". . . and the Lord...brought her to the man"* (Genesis 2:22). Once God made Adam aware of his real need, He brought to him someone like him with whom he could relate. Ultimately all our needs are met by God, but He chooses to meet some of those needs through the people He brings into our lives. It is not good for anyone to be alone.

📖 Read 1 John 1:7. What consequences of "walking in the light" do you find in this verse?

....

....

....

....

....

One of the consequences of being in right relationship with God is that we are pursuing right relationships with one another. Conversely, if we are not seeking to stay in fellowship with others in the body, we are not *"walking in the Light"* of Jesus. The word "fellowship" here in 1 John is in the present tense in the original Greek. This means we are to maintain ongoing, continuous fellowship with one another. Either all is to be right in our relationships with one another, or we should be seeking to do what we can to make them right. Unfortunately, a lack of forgiveness is one of the main interrupters of Christian fellowship.

". . . we are members of one another." (Ephesians 4:25)

📖 Compare the statement in Ephesians 4:25: *"we are members of one another"* with the warning in Ephesians 4:26–27 and write your thoughts on the cost of interpersonal conflict on relationships.

Paul warns the Ephesians, *"Be angry, and yet do not sin; do not let the sun go down on your anger, and do not give the devil an opportunity"* (Ephesians 4:26–27). Unresolved conflict with one another gives an opportunity for the devil to have his way instead of Christ being exalted in our relationships. There will be conflict and even flashes of anger, but they must be dealt with quickly or else the devil will use the offenses to divide the body.

📖 Look at 1 John 3:11. What is the objective for each of us in the body of Christ, and how might unresolved conflict get in the way of that?

Throughout his life, the apostle John keeps reminding others of Jesus' "new commandment." In 1 John 3:11 he repeats, *"For this is the message which you have heard from the beginning, that we should love one another."* We are not loving one another if we neglect to deal with any interruption in the healthy fellowship the Lord wants us to have. God wants His body to be a community that works hard at working things out with each other.

If the "One Anothers" are defining our relationship with the body of Christ, then hindered fellowship with them is hindered fellowship with Him.

📖 Study Jesus' words in Matthew 5:23–24. How might our relationships with one another affect our relationship with God?

_____

_____

_____

In Matthew 5:23–24 Jesus addresses the correlation between our vertical relationship with God and our horizontal relationships with one another. He instructs, *"Therefore if you are presenting your offering at the altar, and there remember that your brother has something against you, leave your offering there before the altar and go; first be reconciled to your brother, and then come and present your offering."* The implication is that someone is trying to atone for sins against their brother or sister by making offerings to God. Jesus makes it clear that the offering will mean nothing unless things are first made right with our brother or sister.

If the "One Anothers" are defining our relationship with the body of Christ, then hindered fellowship with them is hindered fellowship with Him. Did you notice where the offense lies in this situation? Jesus says if *"your brother has something against you,"* be reconciled. Not only must we forgive one another when we are offended, we must actively seek forgiveness from those we offend. Have you offended a brother or sister? The Old Testament law doesn't just address our relationship with God; it guides our relationships with one another. In Leviticus 19:11 we read, *"You shall not steal, nor deal falsely, nor lie to one another."* Have you offended with your business practices? *"If you make a sale, moreover, to your friend or buy from your friend's hand, you shall not wrong one another"* (Leviticus 25:14). These horizontal dealings are spiritual matters. Leviticus 25:17 advises, *"So you shall not wrong one another, but you shall fear your God; for I am the Lord your God."* Offering marital advice, Peter admonishes, *"You husbands in the same way, live with your wives in an understanding way, as with someone weaker, since she is a woman; and show her honor as a fellow heir of the grace of life, so that .your prayers will not be hindered"* (1 Peter 3:7). He literally refers to the wife as a *"weaker vessel"*—not any less valuable, but like a fine china cup that is easily damaged by mishandling. In the vernacular of Peter's culture, this is a more affirming view in contrast to the norm of disregarding a woman's feelings. If a husband offends his wife, even if it is unintentional, he must make things right, or it will get in the way of his communion with God. Clearly, there is a correlation between our human relationships and our fellowship with God. We need to forgive one another, and we need to seek forgiveness from one another.

DAY TWO

BE AT PEACE WITH ONE ANOTHER

In Mark 9:50 we read, *"Salt is good; but if the salt becomes unsalty, with what will you make it salty again? Have salt in yourselves and be at peace with one another."* Jesus calls us to *"be at peace with one another."* To be at peace means to have no friction between two individuals or to have no irritant causing conflict. God wants His church to be a community of peacemakers, especially with one another. If the Prince of Peace rules in our hearts, we will pursue peace with each other. We have a beautiful picture of peace in Noah's rainbow—the visible sign of the promise God would never flood the earth again. As the rainbow was a picture of peace to Noah and his family, a picture of judgment past, and a new beginning full of the promises of God, it is an important symbol to us as well. It reminds us that Jesus bore our judgment on the Cross. That judgment is past, and in His resurrection Life we have the promise of a new beginning and a walk of peace with Him every day. The rainbow also speaks of the harmony that we can know with one another—a picture of harmony with others. God wants His body to be a community that always seeks after that which is good for one another.

 DID YOU KNOW?
The First Rainbow

There is no mention in Genesis of rain until Noah's flood. Prior to that, Genesis 2:6 tells us *"a mist used to rise from the earth and water the whole surface of the ground."* A rainbow is the result of sunlight being refracted by atmospheric rain into the spectrum of colors we visibly see. So practically speaking, a rainbow wasn't possible until God sent rain.

Reflect on the verses below and write down your thoughts on what these add to Jesus' call to *"Have salt in yourselves and be at peace with one another."*

Zechariah 8:16

---

1 Thessalonians 5:13

Romans 12:18

_____

_____

_____

_____

The prophet Zechariah instructs, *"speak the truth to one another; judge with truth and judgment for peace in your gates"* (Zechariah 8:16). Paul charges the Thessalonians to *"live in peace with one another"* (1 Thessalonians 5:13). How can we do that? Jesus speaks about having salt in ourselves and links it with being at peace with one another. What does He mean by that? Salt can only become "unsalty" by being diluted with other things. Jesus is telling us to have undiluted lives, lives that are free of selfishness and self-interest as much as possible. These cause unrest in our hearts and conflict with others. The less "self" we have getting in the way, the less irritant we will be to ourselves or to others. Sometimes as we try to live at peace with others, they are the ones that are the irritant because of their selfishness getting in the way. Being unwilling to forgive one another can be a real "peace-breaker." We can't control the actions of others, but we are responsible for ourselves. Remember what Paul says: *"If possible, so far as it depends on you, be at peace with all men"* (Romans 12:18).

📖 In the Sermon on the Mount Jesus said, *"Blessed are the peacemakers, for they shall be called sons of God"* (Matthew 5:9). How does this attribute of being a peacemaker associate us with the family of God?

_____

_____

_____

_____

"Blessed are the peacemakers, for they shall be called the sons of God." (Matthew 5:9)

To be a "peacemaker" means not only that one lives peaceably but also that he or she is an agent of peace in the lives of others. In the Beatitudes, Jesus pronounces, *"Blessed are the peacemakers, for they shall be called the sons of God"* (Matthew 5:9). The text does not tell us such a one is a child of God, though certainly that seems to be assumed. The text emphasizes that a peacemaker not only is a child of God, but through making peace others begin to recognize him or her as such. They see in the child the character of the Father. God is pleased when we pursue peace with one another, and let's face it—the body is a more enjoyable place to be when we get along with one another.

Jesus is called the Prince of Peace by the prophet Isaiah (Is. 9:6). Paul prays in Romans 15:33 that *"the God of peace be with you all."* Peace is not just something our Lord gives; it is part of who He is. To the Ephesians Paul instructed, *"For He Himself is our peace, who made both groups into one and broke down the barrier of the dividing wall"* (Ephesians 2:14). Through the work of the cross, Christ not only reconciled humanity with God, but with each other as well. He removed the dividing wall that separated Jews and Gentiles in the Temple. Since our Lord is the ultimate peacemaker, we are shown to be like Him when we exhibit this attribute. God wants His church to be a community of peacemakers, especially with one another.

📖 Look at Romans 14:19 in its context and record what you learn there about this important "one another" command.

Paul writes to the Roman believers, *"So then let us pursue the things which make for peace and the building up of one another"* (Romans 14:19). What does it mean to be a "peace-maker"? Paul clearly calls us to pursue peace, but not as an end in itself. Rather, we are to pursue the "things which make for peace" with one another. We cannot control whether there will be peace, but we can pursue peacemaking. To fully appreciate Paul's point, we need to understand the context. He is discussing the need for each believer to have convictions, not mere opinions. He charges us to use these convictions to guide our own behavior, not to judge another.

What has this to do with forgiving one another? Think about the two sides of the issues Paul addresses in Romans 14. He gives examples of one who eats meat and another who thinks it wrong. He references the person who judges one day of the week (presumably the Sabbath) as above the others, and another who treats all days the same. The destination he challenges them toward is to study the matter fully, for *"each person must be fully convinced in his own mind"* (Romans 14:5). The problem is we tend to make up our minds without studying the matter fully. Paul starts the chapter saying, *"Now accept the one who is weak in faith, but not for the purpose of passing judgment on his opinions"* (Romans 14:1). In other words, forgive them for not having fully developed convictions. If we don't forgive their imperfections, we will find ourselves "passing judgment" on their opinions. Since "each person must be fully convinced," we must allow for the possibility that we don't have it all figured out either.

God wants His church to be a community where we walk with one
another according to love.

But what about when we really are right? First of all, it probably isn't as many times as we think. But equally important, even if we are right, there is more at stake than our rights. In Romans 14:7 Paul reminds, *"For not one of us lives for himself."* Self should not be the only or even the main consideration. If we are right and the other is wrong, and we demand our way, we say by action that the other person doesn't matter. Paul points out, *". . . if because of food your brother is hurt, you are not walking according to love. Do not destroy with your food him for whom Christ died"* (Romans 14:15). If we live selfishly and carelessly, instead of pursuing peace we are pursuing conflict and position ourselves to be the one in need of forgiveness. That's not what God wants the body to be like. God wants His church to be a community where we walk with one another according to love. We need to be working for "the building up of one another." To pursue peace means that even if we are right, we are willing to not demand our rights. Who knows? Perhaps by our deference, we can earn the right to be heard and bring others to a more mature position. That is a worthy pursuit.

📖 Consider the following verses and make note of what they have to say about how us being peacemakers affects our testimony with those who don't know God.

Matthew 5:13

_____

_____

_____

_____

_____

Romans 2:23–24

_____

_____

_____

_____

_____

John 13:35

Sometimes forgiveness on our part will be a necessity if peace is to ever to be a reality. Jesus says, *"You are the salt of the earth"* (Matthew 5:13). The ability to create thirst is one task salt is able to accomplish. Our lives should make others thirst for God. This includes Christians and non-Christians. When we are not at peace with others in the body because of offenses or unforgiveness, we will not be able to draw them closer to God. Even worse, when the world sees Christians unable to get along with one another, our salt (influence with the world) loses its savor. We get in the way of them having a thirst for God. Paul warns the Jews, *"You who boast in the Law, through your breaking the Law, do you dishonor God? For the name of God is blasphemed among the Gentiles because of you"* (Romans 2:23-24). If our faith doesn't make enough difference in our lives to make us at peace with each other, it isn't very attractive to those far from God. On the other hand, Jesus says, *"By this will all men know that you are My disciples, if you have love for one another"* (John 13:35).

> Jesus says, *"By this will all men know that you are My disciples, if you have love for one another"* (John 13:35)

When we show the unconditional love of Christ to our fellow believers, we demonstrate that we are true followers of Jesus, the Prince of Peace. Love is the ultimate apologetic— the proof that we have peace with God which moves us to pursue peace with each other. God wants His church to be a community where we walk with one another according to love while pursuing peace. What is God saying to you about walking in peace with Him or with others?

DAY THREE

RELEASING OUR GRIEVANCES (JOHN 13:34)

When we recite the Lord's Prayer, I'm not sure we understand what we are actually praying. Jesus taught His followers to pray, *"And forgive us our debts, as we also have forgiven our debtors. . . . For if you forgive others for their transgressions, your heavenly Father will also forgive you. But if you do not forgive others, then your Father will not forgive your transgressions"* (Matthew 6:12, 14–15). Do we really want God to show us the same kind of forgiveness that we show each other? The Greek word translated "forgive" here, *aphiemi*, paints an interesting picture. It literally means "to release, to let go." What does that have to do with forgiveness? If you will think back to someone you were slow to forgive or perhaps have not forgiven to this day, you will know that when you have chosen not to forgive you have chosen to hold on to his or her offense. You were not (or are not) willing to *let it go*. When we forgive someone, we release him or her from the penalty we want to impose (or that we may want God to impose). We release them from the prison of our hateful glares or our cold stares or our ignore-them-at-all-costs actions. God does not want us being prison wardens, keeping others locked up in our penitentiary of unforgiveness. He knows that if we do not forgive, we are the real prisoners, bound by bitterness and anger and hate. Forgiveness is really a matter of faith. Can we trust God to deal with the wrong they may have done us, or do we hold on to vengeance as a right? To the Romans Paul writes, *"Never pay back evil for evil to anyone. If possible, so far as it depends on you, be at peace with all men. Never take your own revenge, beloved, but leave room for the wrath of God, for it is written, 'Vengeance is Mine, I will repay,' says the Lord"* (Romans 12:17-19). Can we trust God that if someone needs to be punished, He will do the right thing in the right way? Or do we fear He will choose grace when we want justice?

God wants His body to be a community that works hard at working things out with each other.

📖 Look up Romans 15:17 and write what you learn about the basis of us accepting one another and what results when we do.

_____

_____

_____

_____

God wants us to be "releasers" like Him. He releases us from our sin by His own loving death for that sin. In dying, He paid for that sin fully and now we can know the joy of freedom and of being released to walk with Him in open, honest fellowship. What an incredible gift! He wants us to walk that way with one another also. Romans 15:7 instructs, *"Therefore, accept one another, just as Christ also accepted us to the glory of God."* God wants His body to be marked by showing grace to one another. That means releasing others, not holding them captive to our opinions, emotions, attitudes, or judgments. When we live in such a way, God is glorified in us. God wants His body to be a community that works hard at working things out with each other.

📖 Reread the Lord's Prayer in Matthew 6:9–13 and then record your observations on the contrast between forgiving and being led into temptation.

_____

_____

_____

_____

The phrase, *"forgive us our debts, as we also have forgiven our debtors"* is followed by *"do not lead us into temptation but deliver us from evil."* One temptation to avoid and an evil to be delivered from is unforgiveness, for it leads us to additional sins of pride and self-righteousness. When we stubbornly refuse to forgive, our prayers and enjoyment of God's grace are both hindered. When we hold on to unforgiveness, we cannot in sincerity ask God to show us grace while refusing to give the same to others.

📖 Take a look at Matthew 6:14–15 and reflect on the additional explanation Christ offers for this portion of His prayer.

_____

_____

_____

_____

Of all the subjects Christ addresses in His prayer, forgiveness is the only one He isolates for amplification. Verses 14–15 are not saying that believers earn God's forgiveness by forgiving others, for this would run contrary to salvation by grace. However, if we refuse to forgive one another, it keeps us from experiencing the benefits of God's forgiveness and may give evidence that we are not experiencing it ourselves. If we rightly understand God's forgiveness of our own sins, then we will have a readiness to forgive others. When we make the choice to forgive another, God gives us the empowering grace to forgive. Time with one another is so much better when we are walking in grace. So, forgive one another and experience that grace.

> We do not realize it, but every time we pass judgment on a fellow Christian, we are also passing judgment on ourselves. We may not have committed the specific crime of the one we are complaining against, but by judging another we are asking to operate on the basis of justice.

When the Pharisees confront Jesus with a woman caught in adultery, they demand He pass judgment on her. Instead of answering, Jesus draws in the dirt with His finger. The Bible does not tell us what He writes on the ground, but some suggest that He is writing out the Ten Commandments. After being pressed for an answer, He replies, *"He who is without sin among you, let him be the first to throw a stone at her"* (John 8:7). One by one, the Pharisees quietly walk away, the oldest and wisest leaving first. We do not realize it, but every time we pass judgment on a fellow Christian, we are also passing judgment on ourselves. We may not have committed the specific crime of the person we are complaining against, but by judging another we are asking to operate on the basis of justice. If we are going to demand justice of another, we must accept the same accountability ourselves. Do we really want justice when it is applied to our actions, or do we want mercy?

DAY FOUR

THE CONSEQUENCES OF NOT FORGIVING ONE ANOTHER

One day Peter comes to Jesus and asks, *"Lord, how often shall my brother sin against me and I forgive him? Up to seven times?"* (Matthew 18:21). The Pharisees taught that you only have to forgive someone three times, so Peter probably thinks he is being generous. In effect, the popular teaching of Peter's day is that forgiveness is more like probation—it only lasts if the offender keeps his nose clean. Peter is not prepared for Jesus' answer: *"I do not say to you, up to seven times, but up to seventy times seven"* (Matthew 18:22). The Lord then offers a parable so that Peter can understand true forgiveness. He tells the story of a king who is owed a great sum of money—ten thousand talents. That represents about a hundred and fifty years of wages for a laborer, so there is no way this common man will be able to pay the debt. The king prepares to sell the man and his family as slaves, but when the debtor falls to the ground and begs for mercy, the king feels compassion for him and forgives his debt. You would think someone who has just experienced mercy to such a great degree would be flooded with mercy for others, but that is not human nature. This man finds a friend who owes him a hundred denarii—a trifling sum in comparison—and when this friend can't pay, the man has him thrown in jail. Word reaches the king, who summons him and says, *"You wicked slave, I forgave you all that debt because you pleaded with me. Should you not also have had mercy on your fellow slave, in the same way that I had mercy on you?"* (Matthew 18:32–33). The angry master hands him over to the torturers until his debt is paid.

We probably don't realize it, but when we demand justice from others and grumble and complain when we don't get it, we are asking to operate by a different standard than the mercy God has shown to us. We know we stand before God always and only by His grace and mercy, yet in our relationships with each other we tend to expect and demand justice. James admonishes us to lay down our complaints against our brother or sister. If we demand perfect justice for them, we are inviting our own lives to be held to the same standard. I don't think that is really what we desire. God wants His church to be a community where we are kind to one another, forgiving one another as we have been forgiven.

> *We know we stand before God always and only by His grace and mercy, yet in our relationships with each other we tend to expect and demand justice.*

📖 As you examine the verses listed below, write down what stands out to you from certain phrases that speak of what we are not to do to one another.

Romans 14:13

----

1 Thessalonians 5:15

_____

_____

_____

Galatians 5:15

_____

_____

_____

Not only do the Scriptures give us clear advice on our responsibilities to one another, they also instruct us as to what should not be a part of our relationships with each other. These "nots" in our interactions with each other get in the way and hinder our fellowship. God desires that we clean these "nots" out of our relationships. We learn from Romans 14:13 that one act to avoid is judging one another. Paul writes, _"Therefore let us not judge one another anymore, but rather determine this—not to put an obstacle or a stumbling block in a brother's way."_ In essence what Paul is saying is, "instead of worrying about what someone else is doing, you ought to be worrying about your own behavior and how to not give cause for others to judge you!"

Paul has much to say about what should not be part of our relationships with one another. In 1 Thessalonians 5:15 he writes, _"See that no one repays another with evil for evil, but always seek after that which is good for one another and for all people."_ If someone does us wrong and we do wrong back to them, it doesn't make them stop and say, "I shouldn't have done that to them." It just makes them want to retaliate all the more, and the cycle keeps repeating itself. In Galatians 5:15 he warns, _"But if you bite and devour one another, take care that you are not consumed by one another."_ When we seek what is best instead of repaying evil with evil, we break the cycle. The added phrase _"and for all people"_ gives an important clarification. If we only seek the best of the offending person, it could be mere appeasement. There are times when we need to confront evil for the sake of preventing it from hurting others. Even then, we cannot address evil with evil. If we have not first forgiven the offender, we give place in our hearts for evil.

📖 Read the verses below and summarize the main points in your own words.

Galatians 5:25–26

_____

_____

_____

_____

"See that no one repays another with evil for evil, but always
seek after that which is good for one another and for all people"
(1 Thessalonians 5:15)

Colossians 3:9

....

....

....

Paul adds other "nots" to our One Another list in his letter to the churches of Galatia. In Galatians 5:26 we read, *"Let us not become boastful, challenging one another, envying one another."* To be boastful is the attitude of thinking more highly of ourselves than we should, which says without merit, "I'm the one who is right." To challenge one another communicates we know with certainty, "You are the wrong one." The original Greek word translated "challenging" literally means "to call before" and has the idea of making someone answer to you. To envy is the attitude of coveting another's success and saying, "You are right, but I wish it was me instead." All of these wrongs Paul places in contrast to walking *"by the Spirit"* (Galatians 5:25).

To the Colossians Paul admonishes, *"...put them all aside: anger, wrath, malice, slander, and abusive speech from your mouth. Do not lie to one another, since you laid aside the old self with its evil practices"* (Colossians 3:9). All of these sinful attitudes and actions can grow in a heart that refuses to forgive. Think about how Paul expresses this. They already laid aside the old self with its evil practices at salvation. The fact that Paul is telling them to put aside these evil practices shows that, although we are freed from bondage to our old nature, we can still go there through wrong choices. One shortcut to this wrong destination is unforgiveness. The very fact that we are instructed not to do these things indicates that within the power of God's Spirit directing our lives, we have the ability to lay these things aside. It becomes an issue of the will—"Am I willing to surrender my rights and desires to God's will for my relationships?" As we choose to act in accordance with God's revealed will (Scripture) we can trust that blessing will follow. If we walk after the flesh, we hurt one another, and we fail to minister to one another as we should.

📖 Look over James 5:9 and make your observations on what is not to be a part of our relationships with "one another" in the body of Christ.

....

....

....

....

Not all the "one another" commands of Scripture are positive. Our Lord's half-brother, James, wrote, *"Do not complain, brethren, against one another, that you yourselves may not be judged; behold, the Judge is standing right at the door"* (James 5:9). Earlier in his letter, James writes, *"So speak and so act as those who are to be judged by the law of liberty. For judgment will be merciless to one who has shown no mercy; mercy triumphs over justice"* (2:12–13). A right relationship with God hinges on His forgiving our sins, but the outflow of that should be forgiving our brother or sister. God wants His body to be a community that shows one another the same grace He shows us, and leaves judgment to Him.

There are two fundamental truths that ought to govern our lives. First, there is a God. We are not alone. We don't have the right nor the responsibility of autonomous living. Second, not only must we recognize the place of God, we must acknowledge that we are not Him. James further comments,

> *"Do not speak against one another, brethren. He who speaks against a brother or judges his brother, speaks against the law and judges the law; but if you judge the law, you are not a doer of the law but a judge of it. There is only one Lawgiver and Judge, the One who is able to save and to destroy; but who are you who judge your neighbor?" (James 4:11-12)*

The apostle James makes it clear that when we judge each other, we are taking a seat that belongs only to God. He wants us to show mercy and love to each other and leave justice to Him.

Day Five

For Me to Follow God

In a fallen world populated by fallen people, offenses are inevitable. When we hold on to our grievances against others instead of forgiving, we grow in our bitterness (hurt) and wrath (flaring up) and anger (lashing out at others) and clamor (making noise) and slander (cutting others down). With that we also grow in our malice—we want to hurt others or see them hurt to pay for what they did to us. Ours is a sin-stained world, but the church need not be a sin-stained community. Indeed, it *must not* be such a place. Colossians 3:13 reiterates this value, calling us to *"Bear with each other and forgive whatever grievances you may have against one another. Forgive as the Lord forgave you."* God wants His church to be a community where we are kind to one another, forgiving each other as we have been forgiven. Ephesians 4:25 even reminds us of why it is so important how we treat each other: *"for we are members of one another."* But, that kind of community won't be a reality until we first *"put away"* these attributes of ugliness that Paul lists.

Consider Paul's list from Ephesians 4:31 and mark the particular negative areas you struggle with in your "one another" relationships:

___ Bitterness—abiding resentment and blame that is directed toward someone, it is the opposite of grace (see Hebrews 12:15)

___ Wrath—(Greek: *thumos*, from which our English prefix "thermo" [heat] is derived) has the idea of a sudden boil-over of emotions

___ Anger—(Greek: *orgē*, from which our English word "orgy" is derived) originally meant any human emotion and came to be associated with anger, which was considered the strongest of human passions. An *orgē* of anger would be a full indulgence in the emotion

___ Clamor—seems to carry the idea of verbal expression of anger

___ Slander—the Greek word used here is translated "blasphemy," though here it probably means to speak evil of a person as opposed to speaking evil of God

___ Malice—(literally "evil") a catch-all term to wrap up this discussion—in other words, "put away these evils along with any other evils I failed to mention."

> *God wants His church to be a community where we are kind to one another, forgiving each other as we have been forgiven*

How do we *"put away"* the actions and attitudes mentioned in verse 31? The answer lies in the context of Ephesians 4. These actions and attitudes are part of the *"old self."* In Ephesians 4:22-24 Paul says we are to *"lay aside the old self, which is being corrupted in accordance with the lusts of deceit* [and] *be renewed in the spirit of* [our] *mind and put on the new self which in the likeness of God has been created in righteousness and holiness of the truth."* Here in Ephesians 4, the apostle Paul speaks metaphorically of our spiritual state as clothing or as a garment. Before salvation all we possessed were the filthy rags of sin, and thus we had no choice but to wear them. At salvation we were fitted with holy and righteous garments (*"clothed with Christ"*) called the *"new self"* (literally "new person"). Yet in order for Christ to be ours in experience, we must take off the old garment and put on the new. He exhorts us to pull it off the hanger each morning and make it our chosen attire. What is this new garment? It is Jesus.

The Prophet Zechariah cautions, *"do not devise evil in your hearts against one another"* (Zechariah 7:10). Is there anyone for whom you "devise evil" in your heart? In order to be kind and forgiving we must "lay aside" the rags of the old person as an act of the will through confession and repentance. This concept is not simply referring to salvation, since this is written to believers.

Now, reflect on Paul's list from Ephesians 4:32 and mark the particular positive areas you struggle with living out in your "one another" relationships:

___ **Being kind to one another**—this seems to be focused on the actions we express in our relationships

___ **Being tender-hearted**—this seems to be focused on the attitudes and empathies we are to have toward our brethren

___ **Forgiving each other**—this brings in the volitional side

---

If we feel we are lacking in these areas, the solution is not trying harder to be a good Christian. If we could do these on our own, we wouldn't need a Savior. We can't consistently be kind, tender-hearted, and forgiving. Only Christ can make these a regular reality in us. We must "put on" the new garment which is Christ by yielding that area to Christ's control and depending on Him. Part of a long-range plan for victory must also be cultivating a renewed mind—allowing God's Word to convict us of sinful attitudes and actions and teach us to view each area of our lives from His perspective. The application He desires is obvious, but the choice is ours. We have new clothes—beautiful, spotless garments. Yet, amazingly, we can and sometimes do still wear the filthy rags of our old, fallen existence—the rags of bitterness, wrath, anger, malice, and unforgiveness. Our selection of garments is a choice. What Paul calls us to is a lifestyle of consistently dressing in the new garments of Christ—clothing ourselves in righteousness and holiness. It takes kindness and a tender heart to forgive. If we are wearing the new garments, we will be kind to one another, and we will be able to forgive each other the way Christ forgives. What outfit are you going to wear today?

> *If we feel we are lacking in these areas, the solution is not trying harder to be a good Christian. If we could do these on our own, we wouldn't need a Savior.*

Why not close out this week's lesson by expressing your surrender to God's working in your relationships in the form of a written prayer to Him...

NOTES

LESSON 6

ENCOURAGING ONE ANOTHER

Most churches and even most lives are woefully deficient in vitamin E—encouragement. In 1 Thessalonians 5:11 Paul challenges the believers, *"Therefore encourage one another and build up one another, just as you also are doing."* Both of these commands are "present imperatives" in New Testament Greek. That means they are commands to do something continuously. The word "encourage" (*parakaleo*) literally means "to call alongside." God wants us to walk alongside each other and speak words that "build up." The phrase *"build up"* (*oikodomeo*) refers to a building under construction. Each of us is an unfinished project. We are in process, and God wants us to come alongside each other as a help to that process.

We are all appreciative when someone speaks an encouraging word in the midst of a hard task. Work is easier when done with another. People feature prominently in motivating us to do what we ought to do. That is where the two exhortations go hand in hand. We need to come alongside each other to encourage, and when we do, we should build each other up. Paul's challenge is all the more intriguing because he follows by saying the Thessalonians are already doing what he desires. Even those who are already encouraging and building others up need to be *encouraged to encourage*. God wants His church to be a community that is in the building-people-up business instead of tearing people down.

> *"Therefore encourage one another and build up one another, just as*
> *you also are doing." (1 Thessalonians 5:11)*

Unfortunately, it is characteristic of fallen human nature to criticize more than to encourage. There are even more negative words for emotions in our vocabulary than positive ones. Penn State linguistics professor Robert Schrauf researched the vocabularies of two different age groups in two different languages and cultures and found this surprising result:

> "Half of all the words that people produce from their working vocabulary to express emotion are negative . . . 30% are positive and 20% are neutral. And every single one of these groups, young Mexicans and old Mexicans, young Anglos and old Anglos, had the same proportions."

It seems everyone has more experience and capacity with the negative than the positive. That isn't good news. Child development experts at the University of Kansas found a direct correlation between encouragement and I.Q. They found that children with the highest IQ's (an average of 117%), not only heard more from their parents, but most of what they heard was positive (86% encouragements vs. 14% discouragements). The children on the low end of the scale (an average IQ of 79) heard far more negatives (27% encouragements vs. 73% discouragements). Psychologist John Gottman tried to predict whether a couple would stay together or divorce based on the ratio of positive-to-negative comments he observed as they interacted for fifteen minutes. Healthy relationships averaged at least five encouragements for every criticism. He predicted those with less than a 1/1 ration would divorce. Ten years later 94 percent of them had. The same principles turned out to be an amazingly accurate predictor of job performance as well. It seems we all need encouragement if we are to succeed. God wants us to speak encouragement to one another.

DAY ONE

SPEAKING ENCOURAGEMENT TO EACH OTHER

It may surprise you to hear that many theologians consider a gentleman named Joseph the Cyprian to have had the most significant ministry of the first-century church, greater even than the apostle Paul. Perhaps this is a surprising statement, for you may be thinking, *I have never even heard of Joseph the Cyprian.* Scripture doesn't spend a lot of time talking about him, but every mention of him is significant. One of the reasons his name doesn't ring a bell, however, is because most of us know him by the nickname given to him by the disciples—Barnabas, which means "son of encouragement." His character was so associated with positively influencing those around him that it became his identity. Although Barnabas was probably a participant in the earthly ministry of Jesus, he is not mentioned directly by name until Acts 4:32–37. From that point forward in the Scriptural record, this "son of encouragement" stands as a shining example of the power of encouragement to have positive spiritual impact. He encouraged through his words, and through a life that consistently influenced those around him toward the same end. It is likely through his being mentioned by name in Acts 4, that he became the initial catalyst for the early church practice of sharing common property.

 IN THEIR SHOES
The "Son of Encouragement"

Barnabas' character is so associated with his ministry that he is known not by his real name (Joseph), but by his nickname, Barnabas, which means "son of encouragement."

When the apostle Paul became a Christian after a career of persecuting the church, he tried to associate with the disciples in Jerusalem, but all shunned him. Only Barnabas believed in him and was responsible for him finally being accepted into the fellowship of believers. That must have been a tremendous encouragement to this unlikely apostle. When the Jerusalem leadership learned of the first Gentile church being formed in

Antioch, they sent Barnabas to check things out. When he witnessed how God was working, Acts 11:23 tells us he "*rejoiced and began to <u>encourage</u> them all with resolute heart to remain true to the Lord.*" He encouraged Paul yet again by sponsoring him as one of the teachers at Antioch. He sponsored John Mark as a partner in the first missionary journey. Toward the end of that first journey, we read that a characteristic component in the ministry of Paul and Barnabas is traveling to the places they had established churches, "*strengthening the souls of the disciples, <u>encouraging</u> them to continue in the faith*" (Acts 14:22). After the Jerusalem Council affirmed that Gentiles didn't need to become Jews to be Christians, the report is delivered by Barnabas and Paul and their companions, and we learn in Acts 15:31 that when the Gentile believers receive a letter with the news, "*they rejoiced because of its <u>encouragement</u>.*" When Paul suggests a second missionary journey, Barnabas wants to sponsor Mark a second time, but Paul refuses because Mark didn't finish the first trip. Our "son of encouragement" so believes in Mark that he stands with him. This must have been a great encouragement to one in need of a second chance. Mark will go on to be the apostle Peter's apprentice and to write the Gospel of Mark. Paul's opinion of Mark softens over time, no doubt at least in part to Barnabas' belief in the young man, and near the end of his life Paul writes to Timothy, "*Pick up Mark and bring him with you, for he is useful to me for service*" (2 Timothy 4:11). Through his encouragement and mentoring of men such as Paul and Mark, Barnabas leaves a spiritual legacy that far outreaches him and outlasts him. We all have the potential for such impact through speaking encouragement to one another.

📖 Identify the "one another" from Ephesians 5:18–19 and some of the practical results Paul identifies from being "*filled with the Spirit.*"

_____

_____

_____

_____

_____

The apostle Paul instructs us in Ephesians 5:18–19 to be "*filled*" with the Spirit of God. This doesn't mean that we get more of God's Spirit; rather, it means the Spirit is getting more of us. We are commanded to allow God's Spirit, who already indwells every true Christian, to fill every area of our lives. If Christ is on the throne of our hearts, all our human relationships will be affected in a positive and encouraging way. We will speak in healthy ways instead of tearing each other down. If we are Spirit-filled, we *will* speak to one another. We will have something to say and the freedom to say it. This probably includes both speaking in the sense of teaching, as well as casually in regular interaction with other believers. The content of our conversation with others will be both mutually edifying and glorifying to God. We are to speak to one another in *"psalms"* and *"hymns"* and *"spiritual songs."* As you probably guessed, psalms refer to the poetic books of the Old Testament bearing that name. This is a collection of 150 songs written by different leaders of the Old Testament era. Hymns are not as straightforward. These are not the songs in your church hymnal—those written within the last few hundred years. The word simply means songs of praise. While psalms are songs *about* a request for deliverance or celebrating God's intervention, hymns are songs of praise *to* God not for what He does, but for who He is. Spiritual songs are literally spiritual *odes*. The "ode" was a classical Greek method of storytelling somewhat like the modern ballad. Paul qualifies this with the adjective *"spiritual."*

What in the world does it mean to speak to one another in such a way? Is all of life supposed to be like a Broadway play, with every major turn of events interrupted by a show-stopping musical number? No, Paul says *"speaking to one another"*, not *"singing to one another."* The next phrase gives helpful clarity: *"singing and making melody with your heart to the Lord."* Our singing is to the Lord. Don't get so focused on the method used that you miss the attitude. We only have a song in our heart when we are joyful. The phrase *"making melody"* refers to musical accompaniment; it gives the idea of an instrument playing notes and tones compatible with the overall song. Think about that. Like musicians following the conductor, what we say to one another should be in sync with the director's wishes. It should not be discordant. God wants His church to be a community whose hearts are in such harmony with Him that our speech to each other is in harmony with His plan.

> *God wants His church to be a community whose hearts are so in harmony with Him that our speech to each other is in harmony with His plan.*

📖 Make a thorough scrutiny of the larger context of what Peter has to say in 1 Peter 4:11 and then write out how spirit-filled speech ought to look according to this verse.

The apostle Peter conveys a similar thought in 1 Peter 4:11: *"Whoever speaks, is to do so as one who is speaking the utterances of God."* God wants to so pervade our lives that in our relationships with one another we say what He would say in every situation. Think of what kind of community the church will be if that is true all the time. We can't control what others will do; we can't even control ourselves. If we walk, however, in yieldedness to Christ—if He is in control of every area of our lives—He will be in control of our tongues. We *will* say what He wants said. God wants His church to be a community whose hearts are so in harmony with Him that our speech to each other is in harmony with His plan.

📖 Read the companion verses to Ephesians 5:19 from the "one another" of Colossians 3:16–17 and then identify what this passage adds to our consideration of speaking encouragement.

In Colossians 3:16 we are told, *"Let the word of Christ richly dwell within you, with all wisdom teaching and admonishing one another with psalms and hymns and spiritual songs, singing with thankfulness in your hearts to God."* As you read this verse, you probably notice how similar it is to the thought Paul conveys in Ephesians 5:19. One of the ways we can align our speech with God's will and purpose is if we are letting *"the word of Christ richly dwell within"* us. The phrase *"richly dwell"* is an imperative (command). The more we are under the influence of the word of God, the more we speak in line with what He has to say.

As with the Ephesians passage, Paul paints a picture of Christians as members of a great orchestra playing constantly on beat with the conductor. When we do this, we are able to teach and admonish one another God's way. The word *"teaching"* means simply "to instruct by word of mouth." When we are under the influence of God's word and in harmony with the conductor, we are able to speak into the lives of others in a way that equips and gives direction. The word *"admonishing"* literally means "to place before the mind." It carries the idea of warning or exhorting. While we cannot control how others will receive our admonishing, we *will* speak truth when led by Jesus, our conductor.

> *Let your speech always be with grace, as though seasoned with*
> *salt, so that you will know how you should respond to each*
> *person." (Colossians 4:6)*

Comparing this verse to Ephesians 5:19, we notice that here Paul substitutes "*thankfulness*" for the phrase "*making melody*." Paul also says in Colossians 3:17, "*Whatever you do in word or deed, do all in the name of the Lord Jesus, giving thanks through Him to the Father.*" While "*thankfulness*" and "*giving thanks*" seem repetitious in the English translation, they are translated from two different Greek words in the original text. The latter phrase (*eucharisteo*) more closely aligns with what we understand as giving thanks. Verse 16 comes from the Greek word *charis*, which normally is translated "grace." In fact, the same word *is* translated "grace" in Colossians 4:6: "*Let your speech always be with grace.*" The literal meaning should not be missed here. Our speaking to one another should manifest grace, and certainly if we admonish another, we should be mindful of God's grace, lest we be stained by pride. We admonish another for their good, not because of our own superiority. God wants His church to be a community that speaks truth with grace.

Not only is our speaking to one another to be influenced by the word of God, it *is* to be the word of God. Paul closes out the fourth chapter of 1 Thessalonians, saying "*Therefore comfort one another with these words*" (1 Thessalonians 4:18). Under the inspiration of the Holy Spirit, Paul begins this thought back in verse 13 with the explanation: "*we do not want you to be uninformed, brethren, about those who are asleep, so that you will not grieve as do the rest that have no hope.*" Paul teaches these believers about the Second Coming of Christ and the glorious future that awaits all who know Him. This truth has to be a great comfort to any Christians in Thessalonica who are grieving the death of some beloved family member. It is of great comfort to us today as well! While none of us can write Scripture today, we *can* speak it to one another to provide comfort and perspective on life. Truth always builds up even if it isn't what we want to hear. It especially builds up when it gives us a godly perspective on the circumstances going on in our lives. God wants us to encourage one another with truth. Who can you encourage today?

LESSON SIX – DAY TWO

THE DANGER OF DISCOURAGEMENT

On one occasion when I was a child, my older brother and one of his friends began berating me with teasing and taunting. In frustration, I ran to my mom to get her to make them stop. Instead, she taught me the proverbial poem, "sticks and stones may break my bones, but words will never hurt me." With renewed confidence, I marched out and repeated the rhyme to my tormentors. I'm not sure what response my mother was hoping this would produce, but I was sorely disappointed in its ineffectiveness to my situation. My brother and his friend picked up sticks and rocks and started throwing them at me. It was a painful life lesson and based on the lack of help to be found in the first half of the couplet, I came away convinced that the second half must not be accurate either. Since then, I have empirically verified through situation after situation that in fact, words *do* have the power to hurt me just as much as sticks and stones, if not more so. At least broken bones eventually heal within a few months.

Words are powerful objects. They can be mightily used for good, but also can affect lasting damage. A young man who is told by his father that he will never amount to anything often ends up meeting that negative expectation. The young girl who is told she is ugly by her peers can replay this negative label over and over in her mind regardless of how beautiful she becomes, and often ends up fighting the insecurity of the lie the rest of her life. God wants His church to be a community that is in the "building-people-up" business rather than tearing people down. He wants us to be a community where discouragement is in danger of extinction.

> *"Let your speech always be with grace, as though seasoned with*
> *salt, so that you will know how you should respond to each per-*
> *son." (Colossians 4:6)*

📖 What do the statements of James 3:3–5 imply about the potential influence of our tongues and words on others?

To talk about the prominence of the tongue, James relates three illustrations from life. They share in common that with each illustration, though the object of the tongue is small, it has a very great impact. Sometimes the result is positive while other times it is negative. In the same way, our speech can be used for both good or bad. As Proverbs 18:21 relates, *"Death and life are in the power of the tongue."* The third analogy, fire, seems to underscore the dichotomy. Fire can be very useful for cooking and heating when well-managed, but if allowed to operate out of control, it can be quite destructive. As James interprets his point, *"So also the tongue is a small part of the body, and yet it boasts of great things. See how great a forest is set aflame by such a small fire!"* It is worth noticing that in the two positive examples he uses (a bit in a horse's mouth, and a ship's rudder), both have someone else in control. When self dominates our speech, we will discourage and tear down, but when Christ is in control of our words, our speech will encourage and build up.

📖 What do we learn from the "one another" of Hebrews 3:13 about the impact of a lack of encouragement on those in our fellowship?

One of the enemy's greatest tools is discouragement. The writer of Hebrews implores us, *"But encourage one another day after day, as long as it is still called 'Today,' so that none of you will be hardened by the deceitfulness of sin."* In a vacuum of encouragement Satan goes to work. He knows that if he can discourage us, even if he can't stop us, he can at least slow us down. But God has designed the body so that we have the right, ability, and responsibility to help each other avoid discouragement. Ecclesiastes 4:9–10 tells us, *"Two are better than one because they have a good return for their labor, for if either of them falls, the one will lift up his companion. But woe to the one who falls when there is not another to lift him up."* God wants His body to be a community where discouragement is in danger of extinction. He wants us so connected to each other that there is always another to lift us up and encourage us when we fall prey to the enemy's darts of discouragement.

> *"But encourage one another day after day, as long as it is still called 'Today,' so that none of you will be hardened by the deceitfulness of sin." (Hebrews 3:13)*

What are we called to do in Hebrews 3:13? We are to *"encourage one another"*—to come along side each other. Who are we to encourage? Don't miss the obvious here—we are to encourage *"one another."* Encouragement is a two-way street. We should be giving it *and* receiving it. If you are feeling the need for encouragement, you may find it easy to overlook that someone around you needs it too. Maybe they won't be able to reciprocate right away, but your gift of encouragement when they need it will be repaid many times. You can encourage others in trust that in God's time He will send someone to encourage you as well. In the meantime, it may help to get your eyes off yourself.

How often are we to encourage one another? We are to encourage *"day after day."* This call from the writer of Hebrews is a "present tense imperative" in the Greek—a command to do something continuously. We all need encouragement every day, so we should give it every day. When are we to encourage? The author tells us, *"as long as it is still called 'Today.'"* If we are sensitive to the Lord, He will prompt us concerning those who need to be encouraged. Unfortunately, it is all too easy to put off obedience to a task as intangible as encouraging. But the verse tells us we need to act on these promptings while it is still called *"Today."*

📖 Along these same lines, what do we learn from Ephesians 4:27 about the consequences of unresolved conflict on relationships in the church body and its ability to encourage instead of discourage?

_____

_____

_____

_____

Paul challenges the Ephesians to not let the sun go down on their anger, so they might not *"give the devil an opportunity"* (Ephesians 4:27). For the same reason, we should also not let the sun go down on any prompting to encourage someone. Why are we to encourage one another? We need to encourage, because without it, any of us can be *"hardened by the deceitfulness of sin."* There is an interesting reference in the immediate context of today's verse. Hebrews 3:8 reads, *"Do not harden your hearts as when they provoked Me, in the day of trial in the wilderness."* Since there is a *"day of trial"* (temptation), we dare not delay our encouragement to another day or we may be too late. God may want to use us this day to keep another from hardening their hearts toward Him. If so, it is both a privilege and a responsibility.

Jeremiah writes, *"The heart is more deceitful than all else and is desperately sick"* (Jeremiah 17:9). Our hearts can become hardened toward God by the deceitfulness of our sinful propensities. In our moments of weakness, we need those around us to love us enough to come alongside. In someone else's moment of need, we may be the person God uses to come alongside them.

LESSON SIX – DAY THREE

THE PHYSICAL SIDE OF ENCOURAGEMENT

From the beginning of our lives to its very end, human touch and physical interaction are vitally important.

Much has been written about the importance of physical contact in newborns and even the unborn. Research indicates that as early as 26 weeks a fetus begins responding to vibrations felt within the womb. With babies, physical contact accomplishes more than just comfort and support. It actually helps them with such practical considerations as managing emotions and even regulating body temperature. Infants smile and verbally respond more when stroked. We know that proper physical growth of a child depends on human touch as much as its psychological health. But this physical need is not something we later outgrow. From the beginning of our lives to its very end, human touch and physical interaction are vitally important. In her book, *Aging Our Way*, Dr. Meika Loe relates that human contact is as important to octogenarians as it is to newborns, supplying both affection and veneration. It helps the elderly feel connected, acknowledged, and valued.

God designed us to need interpersonal interaction. When we come in close contact with other human beings, no matter how slight the contact, a chemical reaction occurs. Our bodies release the hormone *oxytocin*. It is a neurotransmitter that is produced by the hypothalamus and is transported and secreted by the pituitary gland. When it is released in certain parts of the brain, it can impact emotional, cognitive, and social behaviors. It has been shown to contribute to relaxation, trust, and psychological stability. It also seems to reduce stress and anxiety. There is a social function to this important hormone as well. Science suggests that it impacts social recognition, bonding, the creation of group memories, and other important social functions. When we talk about the important biblical call to encourage one another, words are not the only tools in our arsenal.

📖 What do you see as the practical implications of the physical touch referenced in the "one another" verses listed below?

1 Peter 5:14

_____

_____

_____

Romans 16:16

_____

_____

_____

1 Corinthians 16:20

_____

_____

_____

2 Corinthians 13:12

_____

_____

_____

1 Thessalonians 5:26

_____

_____

_____

You have surely come across the exhortation to *"Greet one another with a kiss"* as you read your Bible. It appears in 1 Peter 5:14 where we read, *"Greet one another with a kiss of love. Peace be to you all who are in Christ."* In addition to 1 Peter, it appears in Romans 16:16, 1 Corinthians 16:20, 2 Corinthians 13:12, and 1 Thessalonians 5:26. While it is easy to casually dismiss such urgings as insignificant add-ons to close out an epistle, it would be wrong of us to take them less than literally. Culturally, these expressions in biblical times seem to have been reserved primarily for members of the same sex. Though we may not exercise the exact practice today as it was done in the past, we should not dismiss the value it represents. Perhaps in your culture it is more common to shake hands or even to give a hug or pat on the back, but however it is expressed, clearly these verses represent a biblical call to physical encouragement.

"Greet one another with a kiss of love." (1 Peter 5:14)

📖 Read Acts 20:37 and record all the physical interactions that are expressed in the apostle Paul's farewell to the Ephesian elders.

We are told in Acts 20:37 that on their final parting, the Ephesian elders *"began to weep aloud and embraced Paul, and repeatedly kissed him."* It is a normal and natural part of biblical culture to greet one another physically with a kiss. The Old Testament is full of examples dating back to ancient times of such a greeting as a kiss being shared between parents and children, between siblings, and between friends. Solomon writes, *"He kisses the lips who gives a right answer"* (Proverbs 24:26). As you probably already assume, this is not referring to a romantic or sensual kiss.

The word translated *"love"* in 1 Peter 5, *"Greet one another with a kiss of love"* is *agape*: selfless, unconditional, committed love. Many of the biblical passages that reference this practice include the adjective *"holy,"* making clear that there is nothing inappropriate associated with the action. The purpose behind this cultural practice is to encourage and express an affectionate commitment to each other. This reality must make it all the more painful for our Lord when Judas chose this method to betray Him. Proverbs 27: 6 states, *"deceitful are the kisses of an enemy."* The devil loves to pervert what God intends to be a good thing.

While we may not kiss each other, we do still practice physical encouragement. We shake hands. We give each other hugs. We pat each other on the back. But perhaps we never stop to think about how important *and how biblical* such practices are. The idea appears often enough in Scripture that it cannot be overlooked. God wants His church to be a community that expresses a holy affection for one another. Communication is far more than mere words. There are some things that can only be communicated by actions. The biblical frequency of such practices seems to underscore that we all need to be touched. For some, church may be the only place anyone ever offers such encouragement.

📖 Look over John 13:1–5. What do you learn from looking at these familiar verses in light of this week's conversation?

_____

_____

_____

*God wants His church to be a community that expresses a holy
affection for one another.*

Our Lord modeled physical and non-verbal encouragement when He wept. In scripture, He often uses touch to heal. Perhaps the most memorable example of physical and non-verbal encouragement is when He washes the disciples' feet in the Upper Room. This is not mere symbolism. In a dusty culture where you walked nearly everywhere, dirty feet were the norm, and the need for them to be washed was universal. Jesus knelt at the feet of His followers, bathed their feet in a basin, and then gently wiped them with a towel. It was an everyday occurrence, and the practice probably felt good to path-worn feet. The only thing unusual about the story is who is washing the feet. Jesus, the leader, is taking the role normally reserved for a servant. He is making the point that it is right and appropriate to serve one another even in physical ways. In John 13:14 He instructs the disciples, *"If I then, the Lord and the Teacher, washed your feet, you also ought to wash one another's feet."*

Maybe foot-washing seems strange today because it doesn't fill the same practical purpose, but there are physical ways we can encourage each other without saying a word. God wants His body to be a community that expresses a holy affection for one another. Today, look for an opportunity to reach out and touch someone. It is sure to encourage!

LESSON SIX – DAY FOUR

THE ENCOURAGEMENT OF HUMILITY AND ACCOUNTABILITY

We have talked a lot about practical actions we can take to be an encouragement, but thus far our focus has been focused on *what we do*. Another facet of our ability to be an encouragement is more fundamental than that. We encourage others by things that we do, but also just by *who we are*—the example we set. The encouragement is especially impactful when we clothe it with humility. Saint Augustine of Hippo said, "Humility must accompany all our actions, must be with us everywhere; for as soon as we glory in our good works they are of no further value to our advancement in virtue." The world tells us we should seek after power, money, accomplishment, and success, while our Lord calls us to seek surrender and service with humility. We are to leave the other matters to Him and His sovereign wisdom.

In Matthew 6:1, part of the Sermon on the Mount, Jesus cautioned His audience, *"Beware of practicing your righteousness before men to be noticed by them; otherwise you have no reward with your Father who is in heaven."* It is a radical thought, but wholly true, that the right thing done in the wrong way ends up not being the right thing at all. Even the most spiritual of activities can be stained and rendered impotent when they are accompanied with a wrong attitude. In the context of Matthew 6 that follows His statement, Jesus addresses three religious activities which were very familiar to His audience. He mentions giving to the poor, praying, and religious fasting. While in and of themselves, each of these activities would seem to be pious and devout, the problem Christ identifies is that when they are performed from a motive to draw attention to ourselves and to be noticed, they are of no spiritual benefit and receive no reward from heaven. Conversely, when they please God and are the right thing to do—when our heavenly Father is the audience—there is great reward.

> *"Humility must accompany all our actions, must be with us everywhere; for as soon as we glory in our good works they are of no further value to our advancement in virtue."*
>
> —Saint Augustine of Hippo

📖 What do you see revealed in the "one another" found in 1 Peter 5:5 about how each of us are to clothe ourselves, and what do you think this means practically?

_____

_____

_____

_____

_____

"God is opposed to the proud," Peter tells us, and the rest of us don't like proud people very much either. No one enjoys being around people who are full of themselves. On the flip side though, there is something inherently attractive and encouraging about humility. Peter addresses his exhortation not just to the leaders he addresses earlier in the chapter, nor to the younger men who receive a specific instruction at the beginning of this verse, but to everyone. To each of us he offers the charge, *"clothe yourselves with humility toward one another."* The Greek word translated *"clothe yourselves"* is sometimes used of a slave who ties on an apron. We are meant to wear humility like a garment and fasten it tight, so it doesn't come off. This attribute is even more desirable in someone who serves as a spiritual leader and is equally appropriate.

📖 What does Philippians 2:5 say about the attitude that ought to be behind all our activities?

_____

_____

_____

_____

_____

_____

Paul exhorts us in Philippians 2:5 us to *"have this attitude in yourselves which was also in Christ Jesus"* and then goes on to describe its parameters with phrases like *"emptied Himself,"* *"taking the form of a bond-servant,"* and *"He humbled Himself."* If Christ clothed Himself with humility, it drives home how inappropriate it is for any of us to be clothed with pride. In Mosaic Law, God instructs Israel, *"you shall not rule with severity over one another"* (Leviticus 25:46). Even if we are placed as a leader over another, we should exercise that role with humility. In the same context as our earlier verse, Peter exhorts leaders to: *"be examples to the flock"* (1 Peter 5:3). If we all are to clothe ourselves with humility, leaders ought to set the example. Each of us encourages others toward humility when we first exhibit it ourselves.

📖 Read the "one another" of Ephesians 5:21 in its larger context and write down your thoughts on what it means practically.

_____

_____

_____

_____

_____

"Be subject to one another in the fear of Christ." (Ephesians 5:21)

We should notice that in the latter part of the chapter Paul discusses the leadership roles at home and at work. He speaks of wives being subject to husbands, children obeying and honoring parents, and slaves (their culture's equivalent of employees) being obedient to their masters. Before he addresses any of these, however, Paul instructs the Ephesians, *"and be subject to one another in the fear of Christ."* This powerful statement transforms each of the authority relationships he addresses into a two-way street. Husbands who are subject (accountable) to their wives will nourish and cherish their wives and lead in the sacrificial love of Christ. Such husbands will be easy to submit to and respect. Fathers who are subject (accountable) to their children will not provoke them to anger and will raise them with the discipline and instruction of the Lord. Masters who are subject (accountable) to their servants as brethren in Christ will be mindful of their accountability to their Master in heaven and will not resort to threatening. Such masters make it easy for their employees to render service as to the Lord.

All of us are to make ourselves accountable to each other. In the body of Christ, no one is above accountability. When we voluntarily place ourselves in subjection to each other, we encourage the same behavior in others. The verse also implies that mutual subjection is an obligation that comes with being Christ's body. This statement falls on the heels of the charge in Ephesians 5:18 to *"Be filled with the Spirit."* Being humbly accountable to each other is not something that comes naturally to the unbeliever, but it is a logical consequence of walking in surrender to Christ and being humbly accountable to Him.

📖 What details stand out to you from Paul's "one another" charge in 1 Corinthians 11:33?

_____

_____

_____

_____

What does the encouragement of humility and mutual accountability look like practically? Paul gives one example in 1 Corinthians 11:33—*"So then, my brethren, when you come together to eat, wait for one another."* The context is their observance of the Lord's Supper. In Paul's day, it is taken as an entire meal like its Old Testament counterpart, the Passover Seder. In their selfishness and greed, the Corinthians are turning the Lord's Supper into a fight to see who can fill their plates first. Some are gorging, while others go away hungry. One simple way we can express humility and mutual accountability is to put the other person first.

In Philippians 2:3–4 Paul exhorts, *"Do nothing from selfishness or empty conceit, but with humility of mind regard one another as more important than yourselves; do not merely look out for your own personal interests, but also for the interests of others."* Everyone is encouraged when we live this way. The problem is that humility isn't merely an action; it is a heart attitude. We cannot fake humility. Either it is real, or its absence is really obvious. When we do observe genuine humility in someone else, we see what the body of Christ is meant to be: a community where each of us puts one another before ourselves. Maybe that is why humility has such a great potential for encouraging one another. God wants His body to be a community where each of us puts one another before ourselves.

God wants His body to be a community where each of us puts one
another before ourselves.

LESSON SIX – DAY FIVE

FOR ME TO FOLLOW GOD

Over the course of this study, we have actually looked at every "one another" command of the Bible. As we bring to a close our look at the kind of community God wants His church to be, we want to revisit one of the most important of the "one another" statements of Scripture. In Hebrews 10:24–25 we read, "*and let us consider how to stimulate one another to love and good deeds, not forsaking our own assembling together, as is the habit of some, but encouraging one another; and all the more as you see the day drawing near.*" Just prior to verse 24, the author of Hebrews exhorts believers to draw near to Christ, and in the same breath, he calls us to draw near to each other—"*not forsaking our own assembling together.*" When you place several flaming logs together, you have a bonfire, but if you take one of these logs and set it off to itself, the fire quickly dwindles. As the body of Christ, we need each other, and we need regular times together. Hebrews calls us to a lifestyle of "*encouraging one another.*" The Greek word translated "*forsaking*" means "to desert or leave behind." Hebrews 13:5 employs this exact word, quoting Christ who says, "*I will never desert you, nor will I ever forsake you.*" He will never forsake us, but when we forsake assembling with the members of His body, we are forsaking Him. Apparently, this was a problem in the early church as evidenced by the phrase, "*as is the habit of some.*" There will certainly be occasions when we are unable to meet with our fellow brethren because of illness or travel; that is not the concern here. The word translated "habit" (*ethos*) has to do with our ongoing character. For some, meeting together with their fellow Christians simply isn't viewed as all that important. It is important to the Lord however, and it is necessary for all of us as believers. Each of us needs the encouragement, equipping and accountability we get from others when we come together. We also have a responsibility to impart those same realities into the lives of others.

As we seek to apply the principles learned this week, honestly answer the questions below:

How many Sundays have you missed assembling with your church for worship and being challenged by God's word?

What proportion of those absences were unavoidable versus merely by preference?

What are some of the circumstances that get in the way of you gathering with other believers as you should?

_____

_____

_____

_____

What is it to look like when the body of Christ assembles? This passage paints a portrait of a church where each one is committed to being involved. Assembling together is not neglected. Our participation isn't simply to begin when we arrive either. We are instructed to "*consider how to stimulate one another to love and good deeds.*" The word "*consider*" (*katanoeo*) means to contemplate. It speaks of forethought and intentionality. We need to plan ways to move one another toward expressions of love and acts of goodness.

When you think about it, the idea of love and good deeds pretty much covers all of the "One Another" commands. Did you notice where the responsibility for action resides? According to the writer of Hebrews, we are all to "*stimulate one another.*" Are we tempted to skip church because we don't feel like going or think we won't get anything out of it? We need to recognize that it is not our participation as a spectator that is needed, for that will probably not be missed. What is missed if we forsake the assembly is the ministry God wants us to contribute. Ministry is not merely the responsibility of the clergy. God wants His church to be a community where each one comes together with a plan to encourage someone else toward love and good deeds.

> " . . .and let us consider how to stimulate one another to love and good deeds, not forsaking our own assembling together, as is the habit of some, but encouraging one another; and all the more as you see the day drawing near. (Hebrews 10:25)

On the scale below, try to honestly reflect where you fit on the spectrum:

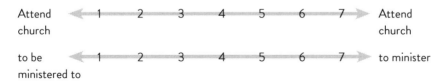

Attend church to be ministered to   1 — 2 — 3 — 4 — 5 — 6 — 7   Attend church to minister

Christianity was never intended to be a spectator sport. We are all to be ministers to one another. That is why the Bible gives so many different "One Another" instructions to all of us. Instead of *changing churches* because no one seems to be ministering to us, perhaps we need to be the ones *changing the church* into a place where we own the responsibility to be *"encouraging one another."* We need to have the attitude that if we aren't there, someone else might not be stimulated toward love and good deeds as they ought to be. God wants His church to be a community where each one comes together with a plan to encourage someone else toward love and good deeds. How important is it for the church to operate this way? It is not a need that diminishes. Encouraging one another becomes more and more important as each day passes. You need to take it as a personal responsibility to minister encouragement *"all the more as you see the day drawing near."* The closer we get to Christ's return, the greater the need we all have for encouragement. Start today thinking up ways you can stimulate others to do the same.

Who comes to mind when you think of those who need encouraging?

_____

_____

_____

What are some practical things you can to do be a blessing and encouragement to others?

_____

_____

_____

_____

Why not close out this week's lesson by expressing your surrender to God's working in your relationships in the form of a written prayer to Him...

_____

_____

_____

_____

_____

_____

_____

_____

Works Cited

1. ABC News, Feb. 2, 2005.

2. http://en.wikipedia.org/wiki/Positivity/negativity_ratio

NOTES

LEADER'S GUIDE

TABLE OF CONTENTS

HOW TO LEAD A SMALL-GROUP BIBLE STUDY

The best way to become a better discussion leader is to regularly evaluate your group discussion sessions. The most effective leaders are those who consistently look for ways to improve.

But before you start preparing for your first group session, you need to know the problem areas that will most likely weaken the effectiveness of your study group. Commit now to have the best Bible study group that you can possibly have. Ask the Lord to motivate you as a group leader and to steer you away from bad habits.

How to Guarantee a Poor Discussion Group:

1. Prepare inadequately.

2. Show improper attitude toward people in the group (lack of acceptance).

3. Fail to create an atmosphere of freedom and ease.

4. Allow the discussion to wander aimlessly.

5. Dominate the discussion yourself.

6. Let a small minority dominate the discussion.

7. Leave the discussion "in the air," so to speak, without presenting any concluding statements or some type of closure.

8. Ask too many "telling" or "trying" questions. (Don't ask individuals in your group pointed or threatening questions that might bring embarrassment to them or make them feel uncomfortable.)

9. End the discussion without adequate application points.

10. Do the same thing every time.

11. Become resentful and angry when people disagree with you. After all, you did prepare. You are the leader!

12. End the discussion with an argument.

13. Never spend any time with the members of your group other than the designated discussion meeting time.

Helpful Hints

One of the best ways to learn to be an effective Bible discussion leader is to sit under a good model. If you have had the chance to be in a group with an effective facilitator, think about the things that made him or her effective.

Though you can learn much and shape many convictions from those good models, you can also glean some valuable lessons on what not to do from those who didn't do such a good job. Bill Donahue has done a good job of categorizing the leader's role in facilitating dynamic discussion into four key actions. They are easy to remember as he links them to the acrostic ACTS:

*A leader ACTS to facilitate discussions by:

- Acknowledging everyone who speaks during a discussion.

- Clarifying what is being said and felt.

- Taking it to the group as a means of generating discussion.

- Summarizing what has been said.

*Taken from *Leading Life-Changing Small Groups* ©1996 by the Willow Creek Association. Used by permission of ZondervanPublishing House.

Make a point to give each group member ample opportunity to speak. Pay close attention to any nonverbal communication (i.e. facial expressions, body language, etc.) that group members may use, showing their desire to speak. The four actions in Bill Donahue's acrostic will guarantee to increase your effectiveness, which will translate into your group getting more out of the Bible study. After all, isn't that your biggest goal?

Dealing with Talkative Timothy

Throughout your experiences of leading small Bible study groups, you will learn that there will be several stereotypes who will follow you wherever you go. One of them is "Talkative Timothy." He will show up in virtually every small group you will ever lead. (Sometimes this stereotype group member shows up as "Talkative Tammy.") "Talkative Timothy" talks too much, dominates the discussion time, and gives less opportunity for others to share. What do you do with a group member who talks too much? Below you will find some helpfulideas on managing the "Talkative Timothy's" in your group.

The best defense is a good offense. To deal with "Talkative Timothy" before he becomes a problem, one thing you can do is establish as a ground rule that no one can talk twice until everyone who wants to talk has spoken at least once. Another important ground rule is "no interrupting." Still another solution is to go systematically around the group, directing questions to people by name. When all else fails, you can resort to a very practical approach of sitting beside "Talkative Timothy." When you make it harder for him (or her) to make eye contact with you, you will create less chances for him to talk.

After taking one or more of these combative measures, you may find that "Timothy" is still a problem. You may need to meet with him (or her) privately. Assure him that you value his input, but remind him that you want to hear the comments of others as well. One way to diplomatically approach "Timothy" is to privately ask him to help you draw the less talkative members into the discussion. Approaching "Timothy" in this fashion may turn your dilemma into an asset. Most importantly, remember to love "Talkative Timothy."

Silent Sally

Another person who inevitably shows up is "Silent Sally." She doesn't readily speak up. Sometimes her silence is because she doesn't yet feel comfortable enough with the group to share her thoughts. Sometimes it is simply because she fears being rejected. Often her silence is because she is too polite to interrupt and thus is headed off at the pass each time she wants to speak by more aggressive (and less sensitive) members of the group.

It is not uncommon in a mixed group to find that "Silent Sally" is married to "Talkative Timothy." (Seriously!) Don't mistakenly interpret her silence as meaning that she has nothing to contribute. Often those who are slowest to speak will offer the most meaningful contributions to the group. You can help "Silent Sally" make those significant contributions. Below are some ideas.

Make sure, first of all, that you are creating an environment that makes people comfortable. In a tactful way, direct specific questions to the less talkative in the group. Be careful though, not to put them on the spot with the more difficult or controversial questions. Become their biggest fan—make sure you cheer them on when they do share. Give them a healthy dose of affirmation. Compliment them afterward for any insightful contributions they make. You may want to sit across from them in the group so that it is easier to notice any nonverbal cues they give you when they want to speak. You should also come to their defense if another group member responds to them in a negative, stifling way. As you pray for each group member, ask that the Lord would help the quiet ones in your group to feel more at ease during the discussion time. Most of all, love "Silent Sally," and accept her as she is—even when she is silent!

Tangent Tom

We have already looked at "Talkative Timothy" and "Silent Sally." Now let's look at another of those stereotypes who always show up. Let's call this person, "Tangent Tom." He is the kind of guy who loves to talk even when he has nothing to say. "Tangent Tom" loves to chase rabbits regardless of where they go. When he gets the floor, you never know where the discussion will lead. You need to understand that not all tangents are bad, for sometimes much can be gained from discussion that is a little "off the beaten path." But diversions must be balanced against the purpose of the group. What is fruitful for one member may be fruitless for everyone else. Below are some ideas to help you deal with "Tangent Tom."

EVALUATING TANGENTS

Ask yourself, "How will this tangent affect my group's chances of finishing the lesson?" Another way to measure the value of a tangent is by asking, "Is this something that will benefit all or most of the group?" You also need to determine whether there is a practical, spiritual benefit to this tangent. Paul advised Timothy to refuse foolish and ignorant speculations, knowing that they produce quarrels. (See 2 Timothy 2:23.)

ADDRESSING TANGENTS:

1) Keep pace of your time, and use the time factor as your ally when addressing "Tangent Tom." Tactfully respond, "That is an interesting subject, but since our lesson is on _____, we'd better get back to our lesson if we are going to finish."

2) If the tangent is beneficial to one but fruitless to the rest of the group, offer to address that subject after class.

3) If the tangent is something that will benefit the group, you may want to say, "I'd like to talk about that more. Let's come back to that topic at the end of today's discussion, if we have time."

4) Be sure you understand what "Tangent Tom" is trying to say. It may be that he has a good and valid point, but has trouble expressing it or needs help in being more direct. Be careful not to quench someone whose heart is right, even if his methods aren't perfect. (See Proverbs 18:23.)

5) One suggestion for diffusing a strife-producing tangent is to point an imaginary shotgun at a spot outside the group and act like you are firing a shot. Then say, "That rabbit is dead. Now, where were we?"

6) If it is a continual problem, you may need to address it with this person privately.

7) Most of all, be patient with "Tangent Tom." God will use him in the group in ways that will surprise you!

Know–It-All Ned

The Scriptures are full of characters who struggled with the problem of pride. Unfortunately, pride isn't a problem reserved for the history books. It shows up today just as it did in the days the Scriptures were written.

Pride is sometimes the root-problem of a know-it-all group member. "Know-It-All Ned" may have shown up in your group by this point. He may be an intellectual giant, or only a legend in his own mind. He can be very prideful and argumentative. "Ned" often wants his point chosen as the choice point, and he may be intolerant of any opposing views—sometimes to the point of making his displeasure known in very inappropriate ways. A discussion point tainted with the stench of pride is uninviting—no matter how well spoken!

No one else in the group will want anything to do with this kind of attitude. How do you manage the "Know-It-All Ned's" who show up from time to time?

EVALUATION

To deal with "Know-It-All Ned," you need to understand him. Sometimes the same type of action can be rooted in very different causes. You must ask yourself, "Why does 'Ned' come across as a know-it-all?" It may be that "Ned" has a vast reservoir of knowledge but hasn't matured in how he communicates it. Or perhaps "Ned" really doesn't know it all, but he tries to come across that way to hide his insecurities and feelings of inadequacy.

Quite possibly, "Ned" is prideful and arrogant, and knows little of the Lord's ways in spite of the information and facts he has accumulated. Still another possibility is that Ned is a good man with a good heart who has a blind spot in the area of pride.

APPLICATION

"Know-It-All Ned" may be the most difficult person to deal with in your group, but God will use him in ways that will surprise you. Often it is the "Ned's" of the church that teach each of us what it means to love the unlovely in Gods strength, not our own. In 1 Thessalonians 5:14, the apostle Paul states, "And we urge you, brethren, admonish the unruly, encourage the fainthearted, help the weak, be patient with all men." In dealing with the "Ned's" you come across, start by assuming they are weak and need help until they give you reason to believe otherwise. Don't embarrass them by confronting them in public. Go to them in private if need be.

Speak the truth in love. You may need to remind them of 1 Corinthians 13, that if we have all knowledge, but have not love, we are just making noise. First Corinthians is also where we are told, "knowledge makes arrogant, but love edifies" (8:1). Obviously, there were some "Ned's" in the church at Corinth. If you sense that "Ned" is not weak or faint-hearted, but in fact is unruly, you will need to admonish him. Make sure you do so in private, but make sure you do it all the same. Proverbs 27:56 tells us, *"Better is open rebuke than love that is concealed. Faithful are the wounds of a friend, but deceitful are the kisses of an enemy."* Remember the last statement in 1 Thessalonians 5:14, *"be patient with all men."*

Agenda Alice

The last person we would like to introduce to you who will probably show up sooner or later is one we like to call "Agenda Alice." All of us from time to time can be sidetracked by our own agenda. Often the very thing we are most passionate about can be the thing that distracts us from our highest passion: Christ. Agendas often are not unbiblical, but imbalanced. At their root is usually tunnel-vision mixed with a desire for control. The small group, since it allows everyone to contribute to the discussion, affords "Agenda Alice" a platform to promote what she thinks is most important. This doesn't mean that she is wrong to avoid driving at night because opossums are being killed, but she is wrong to expect everyone to have the exact same conviction and calling that she does in the gray areas of Scripture. If not managed properly, she will either sidetrack the group from its main study objective or create a hostile environment in the group if she fails to bring people to her way of thinking. "Agenda Alice" can often be recognized by introductory catch phrases such as "Yes, but . . ." and "Well, I think. . . ." She is often critical of the group process and may become vocally critical of you. Here are some ideas on dealing with this type of person:

1) Reaffirm the group covenant.

> At the formation of your group you should have taken time to define some ground rules for the group. Once is not enough to discuss these matters of group etiquette. Periodically remind everyone of their mutual commitment to one another.

2) Remember that the best defense is a good offense.

Don't wait until it is a problem to address a mutual vision for how the group will function.

3) Refocus on the task at hand.

The clearer you explain the objective of each session, the easier it is to stick to that objective and the harder you make it for people to redirect attention toward their own agenda. Enlist the whole group in bringing the discussion back to the topic at hand. Ask questions like, "What do the rest of you think about this passage?"

4) Remind the group, "Remember, this week's lesson is about _____."

5) Reprove those who are disruptive.

Confront the person in private to see if you can reach an understanding. Suggest another arena for the issue to be addressed such as an optional meeting for those in the group who would like to discuss the issue.

Remember the words of St. Augustine: "In essentials unity, in non-essentials liberty, in all things charity."

Adding Spice and Creativity

One of the issues you will eventually have to combat in any group Bible study is the enemy of boredom. This enemy raises its ugly head from time to time, but it shouldn't. It is wrong to bore people with the Word of God! Often boredom results when leaders allow their processes to become too predictable. As small group leaders, we tend to do the same thing in the same way every single time. Yet God the Creator, who spoke everything into existence is infinitely creative! Think about it. He is the one who not only created animals in different shapes and sizes, but different colors as well. When He created food, He didn't make it all taste or feel the same. This God of creativity lives in us. We can trust Him to give us creative ideas that will keep our group times from becoming tired and mundane. Here are some ideas:

When you think of what you can change in your Bible study, think of the five senses: (sight, sound, smell, taste, and feel).

SIGHT:
One idea would be to have a theme night with decorations. Perhaps you know someone with dramatic instincts who could dress up in costume and deliver a message from the person you are studying that week.

Draw some cartoons on a marker board or handout.

SOUND:
Play some background music before your group begins. Sing a hymn together that relates to the lesson. If you know of a song that really hits the main point of the lesson, play it at the beginning or end.

SMELL:

This may be the hardest sense to involve in your Bible study, but if you think of a creative way to incorporate this sense into the lesson, you can rest assured it will be memorable for your group.

TASTE:

Some lessons will have issues that can be related to taste (e.g. unleavened bread for the Passover, etc.). What about making things less formal by having snacks while you study? Have refreshments around a theme such as "Chili Night" or "Favorite Fruits."

FEEL:

Any way you can incorporate the sense of feel into a lesson will certainly make the content more invigorating. If weather permits, add variety by moving your group outside. Whatever you do, be sure that you don't allow your Bible study to become boring!

Handling an Obviously Wrong Comment

From time to time, each of us can say stupid things. Some of us, however, are better at it than others. The apostle Peter had his share of embarrassing moments. One minute, he was on the pinnacle of success, saying, "Thou art the Christ, the Son of the Living God" (Matthew 16:16), and the next minute, he was putting his foot in his mouth, trying to talk Jesus out of going to the cross. Proverbs 10:19 states, "When there are many words, transgression is unavoidable. . . ." What do you do when someone in the group says something that is obviously wrong? First of all, remember that how you deal with a situation like this not only affects the present, but the future. Here are some ideas:

1) Let the whole group tackle it and play referee/peacemaker. Say something like, "That is an interesting thought, what do the rest of you think?"

2) Empathize. ("I've thought that before too, but the Bible says. . . .")

3) Clarify to see if what they said is what they meant. ("What I think you are saying is. . . .")

4) Ask the question again, focusing on what the Bible passage actually says.

5) Give credit for the part of the answer that is right and affirm that before dealing with what is wrong.

6) If it is a non-essential, disagree agreeably. ("I respect your opinion, but I see it differently.")

7) Let it go —some things aren't important enough to make a big deal about them.

8) Love and affirm the person, even if you reject the answer.

Transitioning to the Next Study

For those of you who have completed leading a Following God Group Bible Study, con- gratulations! You have successfully navigated the waters of small group discussion. You have utilized one of the most effective tools of ministry—one that was so much a priority with Jesus, He spent most of His time there with His small group of twelve. Hopefully yours has been a very positive and rewarding experience. At this stage you may be look- ing forward to a break. It is not too early however, to be thinking and planning for what you will do next. Hopefully you have seen God use this study and this process for growth in the lives of those who have participated with you. As God has worked in the group, members should be motivated to ask the question, "What next?" As they do, you need to be prepared to give an answer. Realize that you have built a certain amount of momentum with your present study that will make it easier to do another. You want to take advan- tage of that momentum. The following suggestions may be helpful as you transition your people toward further study of God's Word.

- Challenge your group members to share with others what they have learned, and to encourage them to participate next time.

- If what to study is a group choice rather than a church-wide or ministry-wide decision made by others, you will want to allow some time for input from the group members in deciding what to do next. The more they have ownership of the study, the more they will commit to it.

- It is important to have some kind of a break so that everyone doesn't become study weary. At our church, we always look for natural times to start and end a study. We take the summer off as well as Christmas, and we have found that hav- ing a break brings people back with renewed vigor. Even if you don't take a break from meeting, you might take a breather from homework—or even get together just for fellowship.

- If you are able to end this study knowing what you will study next, some of your group members may want to get a head start on the next study. Be prepared to put books in their hands early.

- Make sure you end your study with a vision for more. Take some time to remind your group of the importance of the Word of God. As D. L. Moody used to say, "The only way to keep a broken vessel full is to keep the faucet running."

Evaluation

Becoming a Better Discussion Leader

The questions listed below are tools to assist you in assessing your discussion group. From time to time in the Leader's Guide, you will be advised to read through this list of evaluation questions in order to help you decide what areas need improvement in your role as group leader. Each time you read through this list, something different may catch your attention, giving you tips on how to become the best group leader that you can possibly be.

Read through these questions with an open mind, asking the Lord to prick your heart with anything specific He would want you to apply.

1. Are the group discussion sessions beginning and ending on time?

2. Am I allowing the freedom of the Holy Spirit as I lead the group in the discussion?

3. Do I hold the group accountable for doing their homework?

4. Do we always begin our sessions with prayer?

5. Is the room arranged properly (seating in a circle or semicircle, proper ventilation, adequate teaching aids)?

6. Is each individual allowed equal opportunity in the discussion?

7. Do I successfully bridle the talkative ones?

8. Am I successfully encouraging the hesitant ones to participate in the discussion?

9. Do I redirect comments and questions to involve more people in the interaction, or do I always dominate the discussion?

10. Are the discussions flowing naturally, or do they take too many "side roads" (diversions)?

11. Do I show acceptance to those who convey ideas with which I do not agree?

12. Are my questions specific, brief and clear?

13. Do my questions provoke thought, or do they only require pat answers?

14. Does each group member feel free to contribute or question, or is there a threatening or unnecessarily tense atmosphere?

15. Am I allowing time for silence and thought without making everyone feel uneasy?

16. Am I allowing the group to correct any obviously wrong conclusions that are made by others, or by myself (either intentionally to capture the group's attention or unintentionally)?

17. Do I stifle thought and discussion by assigning a question to someone before the subject of that question has even been discussed? (It will often be productive to assign a question to a specific person, but if you call on one person before you throw out a question, everyone else takes a mental vacation!)

18. Do I summarize when brevity is of the essence?

19. Can I refrain from expressing an opinion or comment that someone else in the group could just as adequately express?

20. Do I occasionally vary in my methods of conducting the discussion?

21. Am I keeping the group properly motivated?

22. Am I occasionally rotating the leadership to help others develop leadership?

23. Am I leading the group to specifically apply the truths that are learned?

24. Do I follow through by asking the group how they have applied the truths that they have learned from previous lessons?

25. Am I praying for each group member?

26. Is there a growing openness and honesty among my group members?

27. Are the group study sessions enriching the lives of my group members?

28. Have I been adequately prepared?

29. How may I be better prepared for the next lesson's group discussion?

30. Do I reach the objective set for each discussion? If not, why not? What can I do to improve?

31. Am I allowing the discussion to bog down on one point at the expense of the rest of the lesson?

32. Are the members of the group individually reaching the conclusions that I want them to reach without my having to give them the conclusions?

33. Do I encourage the group members to share what they have learned?

34. Do I encourage them to share the applications they have discovered?

35. Do I whet their appetites for next week's lesson discussion?

Getting Started

The First Meeting of Your Bible Study Group

Main Objectives of the First Meeting: The first meeting is devoted to establishing your group and setting the course that you will follow through the study. Your primary goals for this session should be to . . .

- Establish a sense of group identity by starting to get to know one another.

- Define some ground rules to help make the group time as effective as possible.

- Get the study materials into the hands of your group members.

- Create a sense of excitement and motivation for the study.

- Give assignments for next week.

BEFORE THE SESSION

You will be most comfortable in leading this introductory session if you are prepared as much as possible for what to expect. This means becoming familiar with the place you will meet, and the content you will cover, as well as understanding any time constraints you will have.

Location—Be sure that you not only know how to find the place where you will be meeting, but also have time to examine the setup and make any adjustments to the physical arrangements. You never get a second chance to make a first impression.

Curriculum—You will want to get a copy of the study in advance of the introductory session, and it will be helpful if you do the homework for Lesson One ahead of time. This will make it easier for you to be able to explain the layout of the homework. It will also give you a contagious enthusiasm for what your group will be studying in the coming week.

You will want to have enough books on hand for the number of people you expect so that they can get started right away with the study. You may be able to make arrangements with your church or local Christian Bookstore to bring copies on consignment. We would encourage you not to buy books for your members. Years of small group experience have taught that people take a study far more seriously when they make an investment in it.

Time—The type of group you are leading will determine the time format for your study. If you are doing this study for a Sunday school class or church study course, the time constraints may already be prescribed for you. In any case, ideally you will want to allow forty-five minutes to an hour for discussion.

WHAT TO EXPECT

When you embark on the journey of leading a small group Bible study, you are stepping into the stream of the work of God. You are joining in the process of helping others move toward spiritual maturity. As a small group leader, you are positioned to be a real catalyst in the lives of your group members, helping them to grow in their relationships with God. But you must remember, first and foremost, that whenever you step up to leadership in the kingdom of God, you are stepping down to serve. Jesus made it clear that leadership in the kingdom is not like leadership in the world. In Matthew 20:25, Jesus said, "You know that the rulers of the Gentiles lord it over them, and their great men exercise authority over them." That is the world's way to lead. But in Matthew 20:26–27, He continues, "It is not so among you, but whoever wishes to become great among you shall be your servant, and whoever wishes to be first among you shall be your slave." Your job as a small group leader is not to teach the group everything you have learned, but rather, to help them learn.

If you truly are to minister to the members of your group, you must start with understanding where they are, and join that with a vision of where you want to take them. In this introductory session, your group members will be experiencing several different emotions. They will be wondering, "Who is in my group?" and deciding "Do I like my group?" They will have a sense of excitement and anticipation, but also a sense of awkwardness as they try to find their place in this group. You will want to make sure that from the very beginning your group is founded with a sense of caring and acceptance. This is crucial if your group members are to open up and share what they are learning.

DURING THE SESSION

GETTING TO KNOW ONE ANOTHER

Opening Prayer—Remember that if it took the inspiration of God for people to write Scripture, it will also take His illumination for us to understand it. Have one of your group members open your time together in prayer.

Introductions—Take time to allow the group members to introduce themselves. Along with having the group members share their names, one way to add some interest is to have them add some descriptive information such as where they live or work. Just for fun, you could have them name their favorite breakfast cereal, most (or least) favorite vegetable, favorite cartoon character, their favorite city or country other than their own, etc.

Icebreaker—Take five or ten minutes to get the people comfortable in talking with each other. Since in many cases your small group will just now be getting to know one another, it will be helpful if you take some time to break the ice with some fun, nonthreatening discussion. Below you will find a list of ideas for good icebreaker questions to get people talking.

____ What is the biggest risk you have ever taken?

____ If money were no object, where would you most like to take a vacation and why?

____ What is your favorite way to waste time?

____ If you weren't in the career you now have, what would have been your second choice for a career?

____ If you could have lived in any other time, in what era or century would you have chosen to live (besides the expected spiritual answer of the time of Jesus)?

____ If you became blind right now, what would you miss seeing the most?

____ Who is the most famous person you've known or met?

____ What do you miss most about being a kid?

____ What teacher had the biggest impact on you in school (good or bad)?

____ Of the things money can buy, what would you most like to have?

____ What is your biggest fear?

____ If you could give one miracle to someone else, what would it be (and to whom)?

____ Tell about your first job.

____ Who is the best or worst boss you ever had?

____ Who was your hero growing up and why?

DEFINING THE GROUP: 5–10 MINUTES
SETTING SOME GROUND RULES

There are several ways you can lay the tracks on which your group can run. One is simply to hand out a list of suggested commitments the members should make to the group. Another would be to hand out 3x5 cards and have the members themselves write down two or three commitments they would like to see everyone live out. You could then compile these into the five top ones to share at the following meeting. A third option is to list three (or more) commitments you are making to the group and then ask that they make three commitments back to you in return. Here are some ideas for the types of ground rules that make for a good small group:

Leader:

____ To always arrive prepared

____ To keep the group on track so you make the most of the group's time

____ To not dominate the discussion by simply teaching the lesson

____ To pray for the group members

____ To not belittle or embarrass anyone's answers

____ To bring each session to closure and end on time

Member:

____ To do my homework

____ To arrive on time

____ To participate in the discussion

____ To not cut others off as they share

____ To respect the different views of other members

____ To not dominate the discussion

It is possible that your group may not need to formalize a group covenant, but you should not be afraid to expect a commitment from your group members. They will all benefit from defining the group up front.

INTRODUCTION TO THE STUDY:
15–20 MINUTES

As you introduce the study to the group members, your goal is to begin to create a sense of excitement about the Bible characters and applications that will be discussed. The most important question for you to answer in this session is "Why should I study _____?" You need to be prepared to guide them to finding that answer. Take time to give a brief overview of each lesson.

CLOSING: 5–10 MINUTES

Give homework for next week. In addition to simply reminding the group members to do their homework, if time allows, you might give them 5–10 minutes to get started on their homework for the first lesson.

Key components for closing out your time are a) to review anything of which you feel they should be reminded, and b) to close in prayer. If time allows, you may want to encourage several to pray.

PREPARATION OF THE DISCUSSION LEADER

I. Preparation of the Leader's Heart

A. Pray. It took the inspiration of the Holy Spirit to write Scripture, and it will require His illumination to correctly understand it.

B. Complete the Bible Study Yourself

1. Prayerfully seek a fresh word from God for yourself. Your teaching should be an overflow of what God taught you.

2. Even if you have completed this study in the past, consider using a new book. You need to be seeking God for what He would teach you this time before looking at what He taught you last time.

3. Guard against focusing on how to present truths to class. Keep the focus on God teaching you.

II. Keeping the Big Picture in Sight

One value of discussion: It allows students to share what God's Word says.

A. Looking back over the homework, find the one main unifying truth. There will be a key emphasis of each day, but all will support one main truth. Keep praying and looking until you find it (even if the author didn't make it clear).

B. Begin to write questions for each day's homework. Do this as you go through the study.

1. Consider key passage(s) for the day and ask questions of the text. For example, use the 5 Ws and an H (Who, What, When, Where, Why, and How): What was Jesus' main point? What is the context here? Do you see any cultural significance to this statement? How did this person relate to... (God? His neighbor? An unbeliever? The church? etc.)

2. Don't ask, "What do you think" questions unless it's "What do you think GOD is saying...?" It's easy to slip into sharing opinions if we don't carefully guide students to consider what God says. What I think doesn't matter if it differs from what God thinks.

3. Ask application questions as well. For example, "What steals our joy?" "How are we like these Bible characters?" "How can we learn from _____'s lessons so that we don't have to learn it the hard way?" "How can I restore/protect my _____ (joy, faith, peace...)?" Consider making a list where you write answers to "So what?" questions: So, what does this mean to me? How do I put this truth into practice?

4. Include definitions, grammar notes, historical/cultural notes, cross references, and so forth, from your own study. Go back over your notes/questions and add/delete/ re-write after further prayer and thought. Go through your notes again, highlighting

(underlining, color coding, whatever works for you) what you believe is MOST important. This will help when time gets cut short. It will also jog your memory before moving to next day's homework,

III. Leading the Discussion

A. Begin with prayer

1. Consider varying the method - this will help to remind the group that we pray not as habit but as needy children seeking our loving Father Who teaches us by His Spirit.

2. If having a time of prayer requests, consider ways to make it time effective and to avoid gossip disguised as a prayer request. Time management is a way you can serve the group.

B. Start the Study with Review—Briefly review context of the study (or have a student come prepared to do it). This keeps the group together for those joining the study late or who've missed a week. This also serves as a reminder since it's been a week or so since your previous study session.

C. Go through the study questions day by day.

1. You may offer a "unifying theme" of study or ask if students can identify a theme.

2. Follow the Holy Spirit. Remember that you can't cover everything from every day. As you prepare, highlight any notes He leads you to consider as being most important.

3. Watch your time! When you are leading a group Bible study, you enter into a different dimension of the physical realm. Time moves at a completely different pace. What is 20 minutes in normal time flies by like 5 minutes when you are in the speaking zone.

4. Manage the questions raised by students and consider their value to the whole group within time constraints. Turn any questions raised back to the group.

5. Whether you make application day by day (probably best) or make application at end, be sure to allow time for students to name ways to put knowledge into practice.

IV. Evaluation

1. After 1-2 days, evaluate how the lesson went.

2. Thank God—thank Him for using His Word in all participants' lives and ask Him to guard the good seed planted!

V. Begin Preparation for the Next Lesson

Lesson #1 - Community Matters

Memory Verse: Ecclesiastes 4:9-11

"Two are better than one because they have a good return for their labor. For if either of them falls, the one will lift up his companion. But woe to the one who falls when there is not another to lift him up."

BEFORE THE SESSION

- Your own preparation is key not only to your effectiveness in leading the group session, but also in your **confidence** in leading. It is hard to be confident if you know you are unprepared. These discussion questions and leader's notes are meant to be a helpful addition to your own study, but should never become a substitute.

- As you do your homework, study with a view to your own relationship with God. Resist the temptation to bypass this self-evaluation on your way to preparing to lead the group. Nothing will minister to your group more than the testimony of your own walk with God.

- Don't think of your ministry to the members of your group as something that only takes place during your group time. Pray for your group members by name during the week that they would receive spiritual enrichment from doing their daily homework. Encourage them as you have opportunity.

WHAT TO EXPECT

God created us with community in mind. He wants to weave our lives together in such a way that we can be there for each other in our times of need. A Christian who stays in fellowship with Christ will be a blessing to those around him or her. But this can only happen as we stay in fellowship with other Christians. Expect that the idea community and our need for it will be a novel concept for some in your group. They may have viewed the Christian life as simply a personal matter between them and the Lord. Make sure that you guide the discussion along the lines of the Scriptures we will study, and don't allow personal opinions and biases to have greater weight than the Word.

THE MAIN POINT

The main point in this lesson is that God created us to be in community with other believers. This study will define Scripturally what Biblical community is and how much we need it.

DURING THE SESSION

OPENING: 5–10 MINUTES

Opening Prayer – A good prayer with which to open your time with is the prayer of David in Psalm 119:18, "Open my eyes, that I may behold Wonderful things from Your law." Remember, if it took the illumination of God for the writing of Scripture, it will take the same for us to understand it.

Opening Illustration – Loneliness has a wide range of negative effects on both physical and mental health, including:

- Depression and suicide

- Cardiovascular disease and stroke

- Increased stress levels

- Decreased memory and learning

- Antisocial behavior

- Poor decision-making

- Alcoholism and drug abuse

- The progression of Alzheimer's disease

- Altered brain function

These are not the only areas in which loneliness takes its toll. Lonely adults consume more alcohol and get less exercise than those who are not lonely. Their diet is higher in fat, their sleep is less efficient, and they report more daytime fatigue. Loneliness also disrupts the regulation of cellular processes deep within the body, predisposing us to premature aging. Truly, being in community with others matters! (https://www.verywellmind.com/loneliness-causes-effects-and-treatments-2795749)

DISCUSSION: 30 MINUTES

Remember to pace your discussion so that you don't run out of time to get to the application questions in Day Five. This time for application is perhaps the most important part of your Bible study. It will be helpful if you are familiar enough with the lesson to be able to prioritize the days for which you want to place more emphasis, so that you are prepared to reflect this added emphasis in the time you devote to that particular day's reading

Main Objective in Day One: In Day One, the main objective is to introduce the general concept that in community we have a greater spiritual impact on others. Choose a discussion question or two from the Day One list below.

___ What common ground did you see in the first group of Scriptures?

___ Why do you think God is concerned about our doing life in community with others?

___ What are some ways you have seen that "two are better than one"?

___ Are there any other thoughts from Day One that you would like to discuss

Main Objective in Day Two: We learn in Day Two about the spiritual stability that results from being in community with other believers. Check which discussion questions you will use from Day Two.

___ What are some examples you have seen of one person falling and another picking them up (both literally and figuratively)?

___ Do you think of any specific dangers that can result from going it alone?

___ Why do you think God created us with differences?

___ What are some ways God can use us in each other's lives?

Main Objective in Day Three: In Day Three, our study of community focuses on the importance of being with others in keeping our spiritual fires burning bright. Place a checkmark next to the discussion question you would like to use for your group session. Or you may want to place a ranking number in each blank to note your order of preference.

___ Why is it a good thing to have the friction of iron sharpening iron?

___ What are some of the ways God has used other Christians to minister to you?

___ What stood out to you from the instructions of Hebrews 10:24 and 25?

___ How have you experienced that reality in your own life?

Main Objective in Day Four: Day Four focuses on the principle community and the role it plays in spiritual security and protection. In addition to any discussion questions you may have in mind for your group session, the following questions below may also be useful.

___ In Ecclesiastes 4:12, what stood out to you as benefits of community and dangers of isolation?

___ How do you see the "cord of three strands" fitting into Solomon's point?

___ What are some ways the Christian community has helped you make decisions in life?

___ What stood out to you from looking at the examples of Biblical personalities falling as a result of being alone?

Day Five – Key Points in Application: The main goal of day five is to seek to put these truths about community into application. Check which discussion questions you will use from Day Five.

___ Why do you think it is so easy to isolate ourselves?

___ What impact do you see of technologies on the time you spend in community with others?

___ As you look at your Christian life so far, what are some needed changes the Lord is showing you?

___ What other applications did you see from this week?

CLOSING: 5–10 MINUTES

Summarize – Restate the key points highlighted in the class. You may want to reread "The Main Point" statement for this lesson.

Preview – If time allows, preview next week's lesson.

Encourage the group to be sure to do their homework.

Pray – Close in prayer.

TOOLS FOR GOOD DISCUSSION

From time to time, each of us can say stupid things. Some of us, however, are better at it than others. The apostle Peter had his share of embarrassing moments. One minute, he was on the pinnacle of success, saying, *"Thou art the Christ, the Son of the Living God"* (Matthew 16:16), and the next minute, he was putting his foot in his mouth, trying to talk Jesus out of going to the cross. Proverbs 10:19 states, *"When there are many words, transgression is unavoidable. . . ."* What do you do when someone in the group says something that is obviously wrong? First of all, remember that how you deal with a situation like this not only affects the present, but the future. In the "Helpful Hints" section of **How to Lead a Small Group** (pp. 110–111), you'll find some practical ideas on managing the obviously wrong comments that show up in your group.

Lesson #2—Loving One Another

Memory Verse: John 13:34–35

"A new commandment I give to you, that you love one another, even as I have loved you, that you also love one another. By this all men will know that you are My disciples, if you have love for one another."

- Remember that your goal is not to teach the lesson, but to facilitate discussion.

- Make sure your own heart is right with God. Be willing to be transparent with the group about your own life experiences and mistakes. This will make it easier for them to open up.

- Don't be afraid of chasing tangents for a while if the diversions capture the interest of the group as a whole, but don't sacrifice the rest of the group to belabor the questions of one member. Trust God to lead you.

- You may want to keep a highlight pen handy as you study to mark key statements that stood out to you.

WHAT TO EXPECT

Perhaps one of the most foundational subjects we will look at in this study is this issue of loving one another in the body of Christ. Hopefully your people will be challenged by this lesson and will begin to view themselves as part of the whole and interconnected with other believers. Trust the Lord to use the Scriptures we study in this lesson to shape a new view of the church for the people in your group.

THE MAIN POINT

The main point to be seen from this lesson is that our first calling as believers as we follow God and surrender to Him is to love one another.

DURING THE SESSION

OPENING: 5–10 MINUTES

Opening Prayer – Ask someone in your group to open the session in prayer.

Opening Illustration – She was too ugly to be loved by anyone. Dorie van Stone was absolutely sure that this was true. After all, her mother told her so every time she brushed away Dorie's attempts to hug her or sit on her lap. "Why can't you be pretty, like your sister?" she'd ask, pushing her away, and Dorie would once again find a place to hide and weep.

Dorie's earliest memories are of long, lonely hours spent in the apartment while Mother was working. At only six years old she was left to care for her little sister all day. Father was not in the picture, leaving their 21 year-old mother to provide for two children during the Great Depression. Times were grim, and Dorie bore the brunt of her mother's frustration. She bore it, that is, until one day when Mother announced, "Children, your father and I can't take care of you, so you are going to a home you will enjoy." Mother didn't cry when she said goodbye at the orphanage.

If life was hard at home, it was doubly hard in the orphanage. For the seven years she would stay there, every night without fail—*every night*—she was beaten before she went to bed. Sometimes it was for a minor infraction like refusing to eat everything on her plate. Other times it was for bullying the other children. Dorie decided that if she couldn't be loved, she could at least be feared. Her tough, angry facade insured that no one would get close enough to hurt her again.

One day, some students from a nearby university came to the orphanage to tell Bible stories and talk to the children about Jesus. They explained the Gospel, and assured the children that they could experience God's love. "Loved by God?" Dorie thought. "Is it possible that God could love me?" The Holy Spirit drew Dorie, and she prayed for the first time. "God," she said, "If you love me, you can have me." Within two weeks, God brought a new Christian worker to the orphanage. She invited Dorie to attend church with her and Dorie soaked up everything she could learn. The new matron gave her the only present she had ever received, a small New Testament. Dorie read it over and over, underlining and memorizing key passages.

God gave Dorie a husband who loved her and shared her desire to go to the mission field. In New Guinea, God helped Dorie to see that He had perfectly fitted her for this ministry. The people there were often cruel. She knew what it was like to both give and receive cruelty. The people there were unwashed and unlovely. Dorie knew what that felt like, too. She was able to see past those things and identify with the Dani people. She could love them, because despite everything, God loved her. John tells us, "We love, because He first loved us."

DISCUSSION: 30 MINUTES

Once your group gets talking you will find that all you need to do is keep the group directed and flowing with a question or two or a pointed observation. You are the gatekeeper of discussion. Don't be afraid to ask someone to elaborate further or to ask a quiet member of the group what they think of someone else's comments. Time will not allow you to discuss every single question in the lesson one at a time. Instead, make it your goal to cover the main ideas of each day, and help the group to personally share what they learned. You don't have to use all the discussion questions. They are there for your discretion.

Main Objective in Day One: In Day One, the central objective of the study is to make the point that love is the ultimate proof of our faith. Below, check any discussion questions that you might consider using in your group session.

___ Why do you think Jesus identifies loving one another as a "new commandment"?

___ How is it possible to fulfill the whole law with the one command to love?

___ Have you had people in your life that you struggle to love? How does this command relate to those relationships?

___ Did Day One raise any questions for you?

Main Objective in Day Two: In Day Two, we see the important principle that we all owe a debt of love because of what Christ has done for us. Below, check which discussion questions you will use for Day Two.

___ Do you ever consider love as a debt you owe? How does that truth change how you view others?

___ Why do you think we sometimes slip into only loving those who love us?

___ What does the fact that God the Father is kind to ungrateful and evil men show you about your own call to love?

___ How can we pay this debt of love practically speaking?

Main Objective in Day Three: Day Three gives us a sense of how the ability to love others is developed in our lives. Look over the discussion-starter questions below to see if any are applicable to your group.

___ Are you secure in the fact that God loves you? How does that impact your life?

___ What is the role of spiritual growth in our ability love others?

___ How does the fact that love is a "fruit" of the Spirit affect our understanding of how we can love others?

___ What gets in the way of you loving others?

Main Objective in Day Four: Day Four shows us that one of the practical ways we show love to others is by putting others first. Review the discussion question list below and choose any that you feel are good questions for your session.

___ What are some examples you have seen of people putting others first?

___ Do you feel like you struggle with considering others as more important? How so?

___ Have you ever thought about the importance of your intimacy with Christ in affecting your ability to love others?

___ Did anything else stand out to you from Day Four?

Day Five – Key Points in Application: The most important application point from this lesson is that we are not just encouraged to love one another, but commanded to do so. The good news is since we are commanded to do so, we can, by faith, trust that God will enable us to do what He commands. Some good application questions from Day Five include...

___ Overall, how do you think the followers of Christ are doing at loving one another as Christ loved?

___ Are you convinced that God loves you unconditionally?

___ What gets in the way of putting others before ourselves?

___ What are some steps of intentionality that can make our love of the brethren more fervent?

___ What other applications did you see in this lesson?

CLOSING: 5–10 MINUTES

Summarize—Review the main objectives for each day.

Remind them that living a victorious Christian life is not attained when we try hard to be like Jesus, but only when we surrender our lives to God and let Him work through us.

Preview—Take a few moments to preview next week's lesson. Encourage your group members to complete their homework.

Pray—Close in prayer.

TOOLS FOR GOOD DISCUSSION

Bill Donahue, in his book, The Willow Creek Guide to Leading Life-Changing Small Groups (©1996 Zondervan Publishing House), lists four primary facilitator actions that will produce dynamic discussion. These four actions are easy to remember because they are linked through the acrostic method to the word, ACTS. You will profit from taking time to review this information in the "Helpful Hints" section of How to Lead a Small Group Bible Study, which can be found on page 111 of this book.

Assignments for next week: Complete the daily study questions. Spend time with the Lord in prayer. Take an action step on the week's "One Another" focus.

Lesson #3—Ministering to One Another

Memory Verse: 1 Corinthians 12:7

"But to each one is given the manifestation of the Spirit for the common good."

BEFORE THE SESSION

- Pray each day for the members of your group. Pray that they spend time in the Word, grasp the message God wants to bring to their lives, and that they surrender to what God is saying.

- Thoroughly prepare for your group session—don't procrastinate!

- As you go through the study, jot down any ideas or questions you want to discuss. Those, along with the suggested questions listed throughout this Leader's Guide, can personalize the discussion to fit your group. Think of the needs of your group and look for applicable questions and discussion starters.

- Remain ever teachable. Look first for what God is saying to you.

- Be prepared to be transparent and open about what God is teaching you. Nothing is quite as contagious as the joy at discovering new treasures in the Word.

WHAT TO EXPECT

Most in your group know something about spiritual gifts. Even if they don't know their own unique giftedness, they can still minister to one another, because it isn't just something they do, it is part of who they are. You are going to need to help your group think through why we have to be intentional about focusing on others and ministering to them instead of being self-focused. Keep your group focused on the main points.

THE MAIN POINT

The main point to be seen in this lesson is that whatever giftedness we have, it is for the common good (not self-edification).

DURING THE SESSION

OPENING: 5–10 MINUTES

Opening Prayer—Remember the Lord is the Teacher and wants us to depend on Him as we open the Scriptures. Ask Him to teach you as you meet together.

Opening Illustration—In Matthew 25:14-30, Jesus told a story we call the parable of the talents. In it, a wealthy man goes on a trip and trusts portions of his money to three of his servants. To one he gives five talents (a measure of precious metal), to another he gives two, and to the third he gives one. The first two servants invest the money prudently and each doubled their money. The third however, buried his talent in the ground. When the master returns, he praises the first two and tells them that because of their faithfulness, he will give them more responsibility. But the third servant is rebuked, and his talent is taken away. We may not have been entrusted with much in the way of money, but each of us has been given a spiritual gift, and one day we will give an account to the Lord for what we did with it.

DISCUSSION: 30 MINUTES

Keep the group directed along the main point of ministering to one another. You may have a pointed observation that helps sharpen the focus of the group. Encourage some to elaborate further on a key point or ask a quiet member of the group what they think of someone's comments. Watch the time, knowing you can't cover every single question in the lesson. Seek to cover the main ideas of each day and help the group to personally share what they have learned.

Main Objective in Day One: In Day One, the main objective is for you and your study group to understand the calling to minister to one another with our gifts. Check which discussion questions you will use from Day One.

___ Why do you think Peter reminds believers that they have each received a spiritual gift?

___ Can you think of some examples of people who have stewarded their gifts well?

___ Why do you think Paul says "through love" we are to serve one another (Gal. 5:13)?

___ What are some of the reasons we don't "employ" our gifts in serving one another?

Main Objective in Day Two: Day Two focuses on the calling to minister to one another through tolerance, not judging our fellow believers. The following questions may serve as excellent discussion starters for your group session:

___ Why do you think Paul connects showing tolerance with "walking worthy"?

___ Can you think of some reasons why showing tolerance is hard?

___ What applications do you see personally from Galatians 6?

___ What else stood out to you in Day Two?

Main Objective in Day Three: Day Three introduces us to the concept of ministering to one another through hospitality. Check which discussion questions you will use from Day Three.

___ Why do you think Peter places loving one another "above all"?

___ How does the exhortation to love one another connect with showing hospitality to one another?

___ What are some of the dangers of losing our fervency to love each other? (this should be open ended instead of looking for one right answer)

___ What other truths grab you out of day three?

Main Objective in Day Four: In Day Four, we look at the overarching objective of ministering with what we say. Check which discussion questions you will use from Day Four.

___ What do you see as some of the reasons we find it easy to speak against one another?

___ Why do we need to remember that only the Lawgiver has a right to judge?

___ How are some ways we can use our tongues to be a blessing to those around us?

___ What are some of the hard ways we are to use our mouths to minister

Day Five – Key Points in Application: The most important application point for this week's study is going to be owning the responsibility to minister to one another. Below, select a question or two for your Day Five discussion.

___ Do you feel like you have good understanding of how you are gifted?

___ Which of the ways we looked at ministering to one another do you find the most challenging?

___ What are some ways you can grow in this area?

___ Is the Lord dealing with you about any aspect of this lesson?

CLOSING: 5–10 MINUTES

Summarize—Restate the key points the group shared. Review the objectives for each of the days found in these leader notes.

Remind—Using the memory verse, remind the group of the importance of God gifting us to minister to others.

Ask them to share their thoughts about the key applications from Day Five.

Preview—Take a few moments to preview next week's lesson. Encourage your group to do their homework and to space it out over the week.

Pray—Close in prayer.

TOOLS FOR GOOD DISCUSSION

One of the people who show up in every group is a person we call **"Talkative Timothy."** Talkative Timothy tends to talk too much and dominates the discussion time by giving less opportunity for others to share. What do you do with a group member who talks too much? In the "Helpful Hints" section of How to Lead a Small Group Bible Study (p. 111), you'll find some practical ideas on managing the "Talkative Timothy's" in your group.

Lesson #4—Praying for One Another

Memory Verse: James 5:16

"Therefore, confess your sins to one another, and **pray for one another**, so that you may be healed."

BEFORE THE SESSION

- Be sure to do your own study far enough in advance so as not to be rushed. You want to allow God time to speak to you personally.

- Don't feel that you have to use all of the discussion questions listed below. You may have come up with others on your own, or you may find that time will not allow you to use them all. These questions are to serve you, not for you to serve.

- You are the gatekeeper of the discussion. Do not be afraid to "reel the group back in" if they get too far away from the subject of the lesson.

- Remember to keep a highlight pen ready as you study to mark any points you want to be sure to discuss.

- Pray each day for the members of your group—that they spend time in the Word, grasp the message God wants to bring to their lives, and that they surrender to what God is saying.

WHAT TO EXPECT

Everyone will come in with different ideas and perspectives on prayer, but may not have studied the topic in detail before this week. Expect discussion and possibly even disagreement. Try to keep differences of opinion from getting out of hand. The best way to bring people to agreement is to keep your focus on the texts. Keep taking them back to Scripture. Don't allow the discussion to focus in on individual experiences or personal opinions.

THE MAIN POINT

The main point to be seen in this lesson is the responsibility and need to be praying for one another.

DURING THE SESSION

OPENING: 5–10 MINUTES

Opening Prayer—Remember that if it took the inspiration of God for people to write Scripture, it will also take His illumination for us to understand it. Have one of the members of your group open your time together in prayer.

Opening Illustration—King Edward VII of England was the son of Queen Victoria, who was a Christian woman and who reigned for decades. Her remarkable longevity was great for Queen Victoria, but it led to a life of boredom and dissipation for Edward VII, and he became well-known for his drinking and immorality and debauchery. He finally became the King of England in 1901 and reigned for nine years before dying in 1910.

In the year 1910, there was a Christian named Joe Evans who was known as a man of prayer. He was on a holiday in New York, in the Adirondacks, where he had gone to rest and to study the Bible. He was fairly isolated, because in those days there were no radios, televisions, or newspapers in remote areas. One morning he arose and felt a strange and urgent burden to pray for King Edward VII. The burden on his heart increased through the day, and by the end of the day Joe Evans was praying with great agony of soul for the conversion of the King of England. Finally, a sense of peace and release came, and he grew convinced that God had heard his prayer.

The following day came the sudden news, "King Edward is dead."

Years passed, and Joe Evans was one day sharing dinner with Dr. J. Gregory Mantle of England, who was one of the most influential and prominent evangelical ministers in England in the early 1900s. During their conversation, Dr. Mantle said, "Joe, did you know that Edward VII was saved on his deathbed?"

"Tell me about it," said Joe Evans.

"The king was in France when he was taken ill. He was brought to England and there was hope that he might recover. However, there came a turn for the worse. At that time, His Majesty called one of his lords-in-waiting and ordered him to go to Paternoster Row and secure for him a copy of a tract which his mother, Queen Victoria, had given to him when he was a lad. It was entitled The Sinner's Friend. After much searching, the lord-in-waiting found the track, brought it to His Majesty, and upon reading it, King Edward VII made earnest repentance and received the Lord Jesus as his Savior."

Upon hearing that, Joe Evans told his side of the story.

God wants to shape us into men and women of prayer. That's the foundation for all other ministry. We all need prayer and we need to join in the burdens of others through prayer. Most importantly, we need to stay sensitive to the Lord when He burdens us to pray for others

DISCUSSION: 30 MINUTES

Once your group gets talking, you will find that all you need to do is keep the group directed and flowing with a question or two or a pointed observation. You are the gate-keeper of discussion. Don't be afraid to ask someone to elaborate further ("Explain what you mean, Barbara?") or to ask a quiet member of the group what they think of someone else's comments ("What do you think, Dave?"). Time will not allow you to discuss every single question in the lesson one at a time. Instead, make it your goal to cover the main ideas of each day and help the group to share what they learned personally. You don't have to use all the discussion questions. They are there for your choosing and discretion.

Main Objective in Day One: Day One focuses on why we should pray for one another. Below, check which discussion questions you will use from Day One.

___ How do we balance the fact that God is sovereign with our need to join in His work by praying for others?

___ In what way does the truth that God may be using a difficulty to drive someone to trust Him reshape how we pray for others?

___ What do you think about Romans 12:5 as it relates to our need to pray for each other?

___ What does the phrase, "favor bestowed through the prayers of many" mean practically?

Main Objective in Day Two: Day Two studies Ephesians 6:18 along with other related passages and focuses on how we are to pray for one another. Check which discussion questions you will use from Day Two.

___ What stands out to you from Paul's repetition of the word "all" here?

___ What do you think it means to "pray at all times in the Spirit"?

___ Are there particular people you have a harder time praying for? Why?

___ Did anything else stand out to you in Day Two?

Main Objective in Day Three: In Day Three, we focus in on the things that get in the way of praying for one another. In addition to any discussion-starter questions that you may have in mind, the following questions may also prove useful to your group time.

___ Do you ever reflect on the unseen work that your prayers may be accomplishing in heaven?

___ Has the Lord ever convicted you of failing to pray for someone?

___ Who are some spiritual leaders we can pray for?

___ What particular issues do you find get in the way of you praying for the brethren as you should?

___ Why do you think we need to pray for each other from the vantage point of our own needs?

Main Objective in Day Four: In Day Four, we examine what it means to persist in prayer with others. Below, place a checkmark next to the questions that you feel are worthy of mention in your session. Or you may want to place ranking numbers next to each question to note your order of preference.

___ Why do you think the Lord Jesus wanted the disciples praying and waiting before Pentecost?

___ What stood out to you from the disciples' failure to pray in Gethsemane?

___ Why do you think Paul exhorts us to be of the same mind toward one another?

___ What else did you learn from Day Four?

Day Five—Key Points in Application: The focus of the application section in this week's lesson is not just Bible study about prayer but to actually pray. Be sure you allow some time to pray for each other. Examine the question list below and decide if there are any that fit your group discussion for the Day Five application time.

___ Which of the ways to find out about the prayer needs of others do you find most helpful?

___ How could you become more prayerful?

___ Which obstacles were most relevant to you?

___ Why not share with the group a need we can pray about for you personally?

CLOSING: 5–10 MINUTES

Summarize—Restate the key points that were highlighted in the class. You may want to briefly review the objectives for each of the days found at the beginning of these leader notes.

Focus—Using this lesson's memory verse, focus on the heart that Jesus wants us to have —a heart to pray for each other.

Ask the members of your group to reveal their thoughts about the key applications from Day Five.

Preview—Take a few moments to preview next week's lesson.

Pray—Close in prayer.

TOOLS FOR GOOD DISCUSSION

As mentioned earlier, there are certain people who show up in every discussion group. Last week we looked at "Talkative Timothy." Another person who is likely to show up is **"Silent Sally."** She doesn't readily speak up. Sometimes, her silence is because she doesn't yet feel comfortable enough with the group to share her thoughts. Other times, it is simply because she fears being rejected. Often, her silence is because she is too polite to interrupt and thus is headed off at the pass each time she wants to speak by more aggressive (and less sensitive) members of the group. In the "Helpful Hints" section of How to Lead a Small Group Bible Study (p. 112), you'll find some practical ideas on managing the "Silent Sally's" in your group.

Lesson #5—Forgiving One Another

Memory Verse: Ephesians 4:32

"Be kind to one another, tender-hearted, forgiving each other, just as God in Christ also has forgiven you."

BEFORE THE SESSION

- Resist the temptation to do all your homework in one sitting or to put it off until the last minute. You will not be as prepared if you study this way.

- Make sure to mark down any discussion questions that come to mind as you study. Don't feel that you have to use all of the suggested discussion questions included in this leader's guide. Feel free to pick and choose based on your group and the time frame with which you are working.

- Remember your need to trust God with your study. The Holy Spirit is always the best teacher, so stay sensitive to Him!

WHAT TO EXPECT

In this lesson, expect that all your group members will both need to be forgiven at some point, and will have need of forgiveness from others. For some, this will be uncharted territory, and they will be experiencing the excitement of new discovery in the Word of God. Some will be surprised to discover how practical and application-filled this lesson will be. Make every effort to steer the study away from being just another lesson by reminding your group members to look to their own lives and circumstances for how these principles can apply to them.

THE MAIN POINT

The main message from this lesson is that God has forgiven us, and He expects and commands that we forgive others as well.

DURING THE SESSION

OPENING: 5–10 MINUTES

Opening Prayer—Remember to have one of your group members open your time together in prayer.

Opening Illustration—In Luke chapter 7 Jesus addresses the issue of forgiveness. He asks the Pharisee, Simon, a hypothetical question: "A moneylender had two debtors: one owed five hundred denarii, and the other fifty. When they were unable to repay, he graciously forgave them both. So, which of them will love him more?" Simon gives the obvious answer—the one who is forgiven more will love more. But the question is not merely theoretical. Being omniscient, Jesus knows the Pharisee is harboring critical thoughts toward the harlot who has been washing Jesus' feet. As the story plays out, Jesus helps Simon make the connection. He points out that while Simon had withheld the expected courtesies of a host (washing His feet, giving a kiss, anointing His head), this tainted woman has given the extravagant. She has washed is feet with her tears and wiped them with her hair. She has repeatedly kissed His feet. She has anointed his feet with costly perfume. Jesus points out that each of these illustrate the heart of one who is so grateful for the gift of forgiveness. The more aware we are of how very much we have been forgiven, the more love we will have for the Lord. Since the measure of our forgiving each other is our forgiveness from Christ, the more aware we are of how much we have been forgiven, the more capable we ought to be of extending His forgiveness to others in love.

DISCUSSION: 30 MINUTES

Remember that your job is not to teach this lesson, but to facilitate discussion. Do your best to guide the group to the right answers, but don't be guilty of making a point someone else in the group could just as easily make.

Main Objective in Day One: The main point here is that we were created to be in fellowship with each other, and unresolved conflict gets in the way of that fellowship. Choose some discussion questions from the list below.

___ Why do you think it is so important to the Lord that we not be left alone?

___ How do you see 1 John 1:7 relating to our need to forgive each other?

___ What are some ways being "members of one another" ought to drive us to resolve conflict with each other?

___ Did anything else stand out to you in Day One?

Main Objective in Day Two: In Day Two, we focus in on the call to be at peace with one another. Below, check any discussion questions you might use from Day Two.

___ What stood out to you from the verses calling us to be at peace with each other?

___ Is it always possible to be at peace with everyone? What should we do when the other person doesn't want peace?

___ What do you think it means practically to be a peacemaker?

___ How does this issue of peacemaking affect our testimony with unbelievers?

Main Objective in Day Three: Day Three takes a Biblical look at the need to release our grievances and not hold on to grudges. Review the questions below and see if any are suitable to your group discussion on Day Three.

___ What is the basis of us accepting one another and what results when we do?

___ What stood out to you from Jesus including our forgiveness of others in the Lord's Prayer?

___ How does unforgiveness negatively affect our relationship with the Lord?

___ Did anything else grab your attention in your studies of Day Three?

Main Objective in Day Four: In Day Four, we search out the consequences that occur when we refuse to forgive others. Check which discussion questions you will use from Day Four.

___ What stood out to you from the references in Day Four that speak of what we are not to do to one another?

___ Jesus called mercy a "weightier provision of the law." Can you think of some ways this is true as it relates to interpersonal conflict?

___ What do you think it means when James indicates that we will be judged if we complain against one another?

___ What else did you learn in Day Four?

Day Five—Key Points in Application: The important thing to see out of Day Five is ours is a sin-stained world but the church is not to be a sin-stained community. Decide on some discussion-starter topics for the application section of Day Five. The following are suggested questions that you may want to use for your discussion:

___ What stands out to you personally from Paul's list in Ephesians 4:31 of things to put away from ourselves that might negatively affect our relationships?

___ Do you feel confident you know how to put such attitudes aside when they show up?

___ What do you find are some of the hardest attitudes and actions from Ephesians 4:32 for you personally to deal with?

___ Were there any areas in particular where this lesson touched your heart?

CLOSING: 5–10 MINUTES

Summarize—Go over the key points of the lesson.

Remind them that living a victorious Christian life is not attained when we try hard to be like Jesus, but only when we surrender our lives to God and let Him work through us.

Ask them what they think are the key applications from day five

Preview—Take a few moments to preview next week's lesson on Encouraging One Another. Encourage them to be sure to complete their homework.

Pray—Close in prayer.

TOOLS FOR GOOD DISCUSSION

Hopefully your group is functioning smoothly at this point, but perhaps you recognize the need for improvement. In either case, you will benefit from taking the time to evaluate yourself and your group. Without evaluation, you will judge your group on subjective emotions. You may think everything is fine and miss some opportunities to improve your effectiveness. You may be discouraged by problems you are confronting when you ought to be encouraged that you are doing the right things and making progress. A healthy Bible-study group is not one without problems but is one that recognizes its problems and deals with them the right way. At this point in the course, as you and your group are nearly completed with the study of the One Another commands, it is important to examine yourself and see if there are any course corrections that you feel are necessary to implement. Review the evaluation questions list found on pages 118–119 of this book, and jot down two or three action points for you to begin implementing next week. Perhaps you have made steady improvements since the first time you answered the evaluation questions at the beginning of the course. If so, your improvements should challenge you to be an even better group leader for the final lesson in the study.

ACTION POINTS:

1.

2.

3.

Lesson #6—Encouraging One Another

Memory Verse: Hebrews 3:13

"But encourage one another day after day, as long as it is still called 'Today,' so that none of you will be hardened by the deceitfulness of sin."

BEFORE THE SESSION

- Remember the Boy Scout motto: BE PREPARED! The main reason a Bible study flounders is because the leader comes in unprepared and tries to "shoot from the hip."

- Make sure to jot down any discussion questions that come to mind as you study.

- Don't forget to pray for the members of your group and for your time studying together. You don't want to be satisfied with what you can do—you want to see God do what only He can do!

WHAT TO EXPECT

In studying this lesson, you should realize that encouragement is a fundamental need for everyone and a tremendous opportunity to influence others positively. Conversely, criticism alienates and demotivates. The Bible teaches that we need to encourage each other even more as the return of Christ draws closer. We will never outgrow our need for encouragement this side of heaven, and we should view the giving of encouragement to others as a faith opportunity – us doing what we can to meet the needs of others and trusting that God will meet our needs in the process. Assume all will benefit from this lesson.

Main Point: The main point to be seen in this lesson is the responsibility and opportunity each of us has to encourage one another.

DURING THE SESSION

OPENING: 5–10 MINUTES

Opening Prayer—Remember to have one of your group members open your time together in prayer.

Opening Illustration—In the early 1960's, Jean Nidetch, a 214 pound homemaker desperate to lose weight, went to the New York City Department of Health, where she was given a diet devised by Dr. Norman Jolliffe. Two months later, discouraged about the fifty-plus pounds still to go, she invited six overweight friends home to share the diet and talk about how to stay on it. This home meeting became a weekly occurrence. Today, an estimated one million people, from Brazil to New Zealand, come together each week to help each other meet their weight-loss goals at Weight Watchers meetings. How was

Nidetch able to help so many people take control of their lives? To answer that, she tells a story. When she was a teenager, she used to cross a park where she saw mothers gossiping while the toddlers sat on their swings with no one to push them. "I'd give them a push," says Nitetch. "And you know what happens when you push a kid on a swing? Pretty soon he's pumping, doing it himself. That's what my role in life is—I'm there to give others a push." Encouragement is a powerful tool for positively influencing those around us.

DISCUSSION: 30–40 MINUTES

Remember to pace your discussion so that you will be able to bring closure to the lesson at the designated time. You are the one who must balance lively discussion with timely redirection to ensure that you don't end up finishing only part of the lesson.

Main Objective in Day One: In Day One, the main objective is speaking encouragement to one another. Check which discussion questions you will use from Day One.

___ What did you learn about the consequences of being Spirit-filled from Ephesians 5:18-19?

___ Peter says, "whoever speaks, is to do so as one who is speaking the utterances of God" – to say what God would say. How could this mindset change the impact of our words on others?

___ What stood out to you from the one another command in Colossians 3:16–17?

Main Objective in Day Two: In Day Two, we learn some of the dangers of discouragement, and how our words can influence others negatively. Choose a discussion question or two from the Day Two list below.

___ What did you learn from James 3 about how our words can impact others?

___ Why do you think a lack of encouragement can lead to us being "hardened" by the deceitfulness of sin as Hebrews 3:13 points out?

___ How does unresolved conflict affect our relationships negatively?

___ What do you think makes for a good encourager?

Main Objective in Day Three: Day Three introduces us to the physical side of encouragement. Decide on some discussion-starter questions for your session on encouraging one another. Below, are some possible discussion questions for you to consider.

___ What do you see as a practical take-home point in today's culture from the references to greeting others with a holy kiss?

___ What are some ways you have been encouraged by a physical touch from others?

___ Looking at the example of Paul's goodbye to the Ephesian elders, what are some pointers you can glean?

___ What else stood out to you from Day Three about the use of physical touch as encouragement?

Main Objective in Day Four: In Day Four, we see the potential of encouragement to be found in humility and accountability. Check which discussion questions you will use from Day Four.

___ What are some practical ways we can clothe ourselves with humility, as Peter exhorts?

___ What does Philippians 2:5 say about the attitude that ought to be behind all our activities?

___ Why do you think we are to be subject to one another, and how can doing so be an encouragement?

___ What else stood out to you from the passages we looked at in Day Four?

Day Five—Key Points in Application: The most important application point out of Day Five probably is the fact that to encourage one another we must be with one another. Below, check any discussion questions that are best suited to your group for application.

___ Can you think of some needs you have that would be helped by simply assembling with other Christians on a regular basis?

___ Who comes to mind when you think of those who need encouraging?

___ What are some practical things you can to do be a blessing and encouragement to others?

___ What other applications did you see in this week's lesson?

CLOSING: 5–10 MINUTES

Summarize—Restate the key points.

Remind those in your group that living a victorious Christian life is not attained when we try hard to be like Jesus, but only when we surrender our lives to God and let Him work through us.

Preview—Take a few moments to discuss where your Bible study group will be headed next.

Pray—Close in prayer.

TOOLS FOR GOOD DISCUSSION

As discussed earlier, there are certain people who show up in every discussion group that you will ever lead. We have already looked at "Talkative Timothy" and "Silent Sally." This week, let's talk about another person who tends to show up. Let's call this person **"Tangent Tom."** He is the kind of guy who loves to talk even when he has nothing to say. Tangent Tom loves to "chase rabbits" regardless of where they go. When he gets the floor, you never know where the discussion will lead. You need to understand that not all tangents are bad. Sometimes, much can be gained from discussion "a little off the beaten path." But these diversions must be balanced against the purpose of the group. In the "Helpful Hints" section of **How to Lead a Small Group** (pp. 112–113), you will find some practical ideas on managing the "Tangent Toms" in your group. You will also get some helpful information on evaluating tangents as they arise.